Invitation to a
SPIRITUAL
REVOLUTION

Studies in the Sermon on the Mount

Paul Earnhart

DeWard
PUBLISHING COMPANY

Invitation to a Spiritual Revolution: Studies in the Sermon on the Mount
© 2009 by DeWard Publishing Company, Ltd.
P.O. Box 6259, Chillicothe, Ohio 45601
800.300.9778
www.dewardpublishing.com

Reprinted by DeWard Publishing from original printing by Gary
Fisher, 1999.

Cover design by Jonathan Hardin.

Printed in the United States of America.

ISBN: 978-0-9798893-9-4

Foreword

Jesus has been universally acclaimed as the world's greatest teacher and His Sermon on the Mount as history's greatest sermon. Yet, most of those who praise Him do not hear Him, and most who hear His words do not keep them.

It is understandable that few in our generation follow the way of Jesus. It is diametrically opposed to our modern philosophy of life. If the majority of us had been there and actually heard Him, we probably would not praise His sermon as highly as we do. In fact, we just might have been offended by it.

Generally speaking, our generation has an aversion to authority, yet those who heard the Lord's great sermon observed that "He taught them as one having authority." We prefer sermons that deal in generalities; Jesus dealt with specifics. We prefer preachers who praise rather than condemn; Jesus condemned not only wrong conduct but wrong motives as well. We object to "name calling"; Jesus unabashedly named unfavorably the leading religious party of His day. We favor motivation by promise of rewards but Jesus, while offering rewards, did not hesitate to threaten "hell fire." Our society seeks instant gratification while the promises of Jesus are primarily for life hereafter. We tend to think of everything as relative, but Jesus spoke in absolutes. We criticize as simplistic any preaching that "makes everything black and white," yet Jesus repeatedly divided His subjects into just two categories: right and wrong. We applaud broad-mindedness and seek the easy way, but Jesus warned that His way is narrow and the gate is difficult.

How is it that a sermon can be so highly valued and yet so universally disregarded in practical application? The answer is that many consider it an ideal message for the first century, but too idealistic to fit our generation. The fact is that it did not fit the generation to whom it was originally addressed. It was not intended to fit that generation or any other in earthly history. Its purpose was to introduce into the world of human frailty a heavenly government with heavenly goals, heavenly values, heavenly attitudes and a heavenly code of conduct for those who "seek first the kingdom of God and His righteousness."

Jesus knew that in every generation those who would follow the heavenly way would be few compared to the many who would reject it. His concern was not with quantity but with quality. Consequently, He compromised His standards not one iota to accommodate the weaknesses of men or the peculiarities of His generation. Had He made any compromise at all the resulting kingdom would not have been the kingdom of Heaven.

Any faithful interpretation of the Sermon on the Mount must be equally uncompromising. If Jesus did not grant concessions to fit His generation, what right has any person now living to do so?

The Sermon on the Mount is recorded in the gospels for all of us to read. As our Lord's message for all time, it is worthy of serious investigation to discover exactly what He is saying to us. The purpose of the following treatise is to assist in this discovery. There is no effort to adjust or reform the teaching of Jesus to make it modern. Rather, there is a careful and reverent analysis of the words of Jesus based on the author's lengthy and careful study of the text, on his conviction that the words were from the mouth of the Son of God and on his firm belief that their transmission to us was by divine inspiration. In addition, there is a conscientious effort to show how the teaching of Jesus can and must be put into practice in our own lives, in our own generation and in the very world in which we live.

Once it is clear what Jesus is saying we are faced with the most critical decisions of our lives: Shall I follow Jesus or conventional wisdom? Shall I bend His teaching to fit my life or mold my life to fit His teaching? Shall my primary citizenship be earthly or heavenly? Shall I choose the narrow way or the broad way?

How I respond to the teaching of Jesus will determine whether my life is built on the rock or on the sand; whether my destiny will be eternal life or eternal destruction. Jesus Himself made it just that simple.

Sewell Hall

A Word from the Publisher

I read *Invitation to a Spiritual Revolution* several years ago and found it to be a wonderful exposition of Jesus' most well-known sermon. Earnhart's writing is easy to read, yet full of thought-provoking material; it is accessible to the common man, yet substantive to the more seasoned Bible student. I cannot imagine a book on Jesus' great sermon that better combines these two difficult-to-blend elements.

Not too long ago I received a phone call from a bookstore manager telling me that *Invitation to a Spiritual Revolution* was going out of print. I knew immediately that this was a book I wanted to bring back into publication, if it was possible for us to secure the rights. I was glad when we were able to do so and am thrilled to be able to make it available again.

I would like to especially thank Paul Earnhart and Gary Fisher, who were cooperative and completely agreeable when we asked for the rights to reprint *Invitation*. Thanks also to Gayla Wallace, who retyped the entire manuscript since an electronic version didn't exist, and who (with the help of some family members) read her version side by side with the original to ensure she didn't introduce any errors into the book. Thanks also to Jason Hardin for providing us with a final copy edit. Finally, I would like to thank my wife, Brooke. After the layout program I use "ate" the tabs in the retyped manuscript, she helped me as we went back through the entire book to be sure that this version's paragraphs began the same place that Paul's paragraphs began in the original.

Nathan Ward
Co-Owner | Content Manager
DeWard Publishing Company

Contents

Introduction

George Bernard Shaw once described the Sermon on the Mount as an "impractical outburst of anarchism and sentimentality." The German philosopher Friederich Nietzsche treated it even less kindly when he wrote that "Christian morality is the most malignant form of all falsehood" *(Ecce Homo)*. In 1929 humanist John Herman Randall was willing to acknowledge that Jesus was "a truly great moral genius," but then wondered how a Galilean carpenter could have uttered the final word on human ethics *(Religion in the Modern World)*. But many more people have held this sermon in great reverence even when they did not know or understand it very well. It is safe to say that the Sermon on the Mount is the best known, least understood, and least practiced of all the teachings of Jesus.

The modern mind, religious as well as irreligious, has treated this sermon in a variety of ways. As earlier noted, some have rejected it as wholly impractical or positively evil. Others have received it, but with significant reservations. Humanism, at its kindest, has viewed it as a remarkable but tentative moral code wholly separated from the cross or a divine Christ. Religious liberalism sees it largely as a blueprint for social reconstruction rather than individual conversion. Albert Schweitzer explained it as a special ethic for a special time based on Jesus' mistaken belief that the end of all time was about to occur.

Among conservative religionists many dispensational premillennialists see it as another "law" inconsistent with an age of grace and impossible to apply in a sinful world. They await its fulfillment in a "millennial kingdom." The large part of evangelical Protestantism has separated life into two arenas, one personal, the other social. For them the ethics of the Sermon on the Mount are intended to govern personal relationships only.

They deem it impossible to apply its precepts to either business or government.

All of this is to say that we have worked a wonder in our times by taking the most revolutionary document in history and turning it into something tame and inconsequential. The word of God has been severely blunted. The gospel has been trimmed to fit the lifestyle of undisciplined and indulgent men.

There is a real sense in which we have come full circle. The Sermon on the Mount was first addressed to a world in which the Pharisees had succeeded in draining the life and meaning from the law of Moses. We live in a world that has transformed the gospel into little more than twentieth-century civility. For this reason it is the more urgent that we look often and carefully at the one sermon of God's Son which perhaps more than any other defines the very essence of the kingdom of heaven. Here, if we listen humbly, our lives can be transformed, our spirits refreshed, our souls saved.

"The Gospel of the Kingdom"

The New Testament view of the sermon is best seen in Matthew's introduction to it. It is "the gospel of the kingdom" (Matt 4.23). This should serve to make two things clear. First, that it is not merely Jesus' exposition of the law and, second, that its blessings and ethical principles are not attainable by the unconverted. This is a sermon for kingdom citizens. Salvation, not social reconstruction, is its aim and worldly-wise men are destined never to understand it.

Luke's account (Luke 6.12–49) places the sermon in the second year of the Lord's public preaching at the height of His popularity—a popularity He never trusted (John 2.23–25) and which proved to be short-lived (John 6.66). The times seem to have been characterized by a great religious enthusiasm which was both misguided and superficial.

The Sermon on the Mount stands as an explanation of the true nature of the kingdom of God. It is a sermon delivered in history and serves to answer the questions which would have naturally been raised by the announcement in Israel of the kingdom's imminent appearance (Matt 3.1; 4.7). In addition, the wholly unexpected character of the preacher and the sharp conflict between Jesus and the Pharisees was bound to stir even more concern among those who first heard the cry—"The kingdom of heaven is at hand!"

Jesus' discourse upon a Galilean mountainside is in reality no mere sermon. It more approximates a manifesto of the kingdom of God. There is more to Jesus' teaching than this, but here we feel the very heartbeat of kingdom truth, and we will neglect it at our peril. Because it deals with attitudes, the sermon stands both at the entrance of God's kingdom and on its more exalted planes. It is not just meat for the mature, but a challenge to the one who makes his first approach to heaven's rule and righteousness.

Beatitudes:
The Character of Kingdom Citizens

Jesus opens his momentous sermon with a series of eight pungent and largely paradoxical statements known traditionally as the "beatitudes" (Matt 5.2–12). They must have fallen like thunderbolts upon those first-century Jewish ears. A more unlikely formula for success could hardly have been imagined. They assaulted every maxim of conventional wisdom and left the hearer startled and perplexed. In this way Jesus gains the attention of His audience and drives home the essential character of the kingdom of God and its citizens.

The whole world, then as now, was in earnest pursuit of happiness and had just as little notion as men today of how to obtain it. There was no surprise in the announcement that there was true blessedness in the kingdom. The shock came in the kind of people who were destined to obtain it.

The beatitudes speak exclusively of spiritual qualities. The historic concerns of men—material wealth, social status and worldly wisdom—do not simply receive little attention, they receive none at all. Jesus is clearly outlining a kingdom not of this world (John 18.36), a kingdom whose borders pass not through lands and cities but through human hearts (Luke 17.20–24). This altogether unlikely kingdom arrived as announced in the first century (Mark 9.1; Col 1.13; Rev 1.9), but most were unprepared to recognize and receive it—even as they are now.

It must be further noted that not only are the qualities of the kingdom citizen spiritual but they are qualities which would not come to men naturally. They are not the product of heredity or environment, but of choice. No one will ever "fall into" these categories. They not only do not occur in men naturally, but are in fact distinctly contrary to the "second nature" which pride and lust have caused to prevail in the hearts of all humanity.

Perhaps there is no more important truth to be recognized about the beatitudes than the fact that they are not independent proverbs which apply to eight different groups of men, but are a composite description of every citizen in the kingdom of God. These qualities are so interwoven in one spiritual fabric that they are inseparable. To possess one is to possess them all, and to lack one is to lack them all. And as all Christians must possess all these qualities of kingdom life, they are also destined to receive all its blessings—blessings which, like its qualities, are but components of one reward—one body called to one hope (Eph 4.4).

In sum, then, the beatitudes do not contain a promise of blessing upon men in their natural state (all men mourn but all will certainly not be comforted, Matt 5.4) nor do they offer hope to those who seem to fall into one category or another. They are a composite picture of what every kingdom citizen, not just a few super disciples, must be. They mark off the radical difference between the kingdom of heaven and the world of other men. The son of the kingdom is different in what he admires and values, different in what he thinks and feels, different in what he seeks and does. Clearly, there has never been a kingdom like this before.

A Kingdom for the Sinful and Lowly

There have been many approaches to the specific content of the beatitudes. Many feel that there is a progression of thought moving through them which begins with a new attitude toward self and God, leads to a new attitude toward others, and culminates with the world's reaction to this radical change. There is some merit to this analysis, and whether or not such a neat format always coincides with the actual order of the beatitudes, the ideas are certainly there. To a society governed by some serious misconceptions about the kingdom of God, the beatitudes make two basic statements. First, that the kingdom is not open to the self-righteous and self-assured, but to the supplicant sinner who comes seeking out of his emptiness. And, second, that the kingdom is not to be had by the "mighty" who obtain their desires by wealth or violence, but by a company of patient men who yield not only their wants but even their "rights" to the needs of others.

Though not explicitly stated (Jesus was not to speak clearly of His death until a year later, Matt 16.21), there is nothing quite so obvious in this sermon as the central gospel truth that salvation is by the grace of God. Here the dispensational premillennialist is palpably wrong. How could men and women so hungry for righteousness (Matt 5.6) and so much in need of mercy (Matt 5.7) find a place in a kingdom governed by a system of law alone? And who could imagine that citizens in the earthly kingdom envisioned by the dispensationalists would ever suffer persecution (Matt 5.1–12). The righteousness of the kingdom does not rest on a system of law but upon a system of grace. Its holy standards are attainable by sinful men (Matt 5.48). Otherwise, the Sermon on the Mount would be the source of greater despair than the law of Moses (Rom 7.25).

Beatitudes:
"Nothing Succeeds Like Failure"

Perhaps there is no better statement of the message of the beatitudes (Matt 5.2–12) than G.K. Chesterton's curious little maxim, "Nothing succeeds like failure." Of course, Jesus was not speaking of real failure even as Chesterton was not, but of what men have generally viewed as failure. The cross was certainly a colossal disaster by every conventional standard. It only seems "right" to many of us now because we have acquiesced in nineteen hundred years of well-established tradition. It is not so remarkable then that a kingdom destined to be hoisted to power on a cross should be full of surprises and that Jesus should say that only those who were apparent failures had any hope of its blessedness. In the following beatitudes the Savior makes very clear that the kingdom of heaven belongs, not to the full, but to the empty.

"Blessed are the poor in spirit" (Matt 5.3). Jesus begins by touching the wellspring of the character of the kingdom citizen—his attitude toward himself in the presence of God. Luke abbreviates this beatitude to, "Blessed are you poor" (Luke 6.20) and records also a woe pronounced by Jesus upon the rich (Luke 6.24). In the synagogue at Nazareth Jesus had read Isaiah's messianic prophecy of the poor ("meek," ASV) having the gospel preached to them (Isa 61.1; Luke 4.18) and was later to soberly warn that the rich would not come easily into the kingdom (Luke 18.24–25). But while it is true that "the common people heard Him gladly" (Mark 12.37) because the rigors of the poor bring them to humility more easily than does the comfortable affluence of the rich, Matthew's account of the sermon makes evident that Jesus is not speaking of economic poverty. It is not impossible for the poor to be arrogant nor for the rich to be humble. These "poor" are those who, possessing little or much, have a sense of their own spiritual destitution.

The Greek word here translated "poor" comes from a root word which means to crouch or to cringe. It refers not simply to those for whom life is a struggle, but to men who are reduced to the most abject begging because they have absolutely nothing (Luke 16.20–21). Here it is applied to the sinful emptiness of an absolute spiritual bankruptcy in which a person is compelled to plead for that which he is powerless to obtain (Jer 10.23) and to which he has no right (Luke 15.18–19; 18.13), but without which he cannot live. Begging comes hard to men (Luke 16.3)—especially proud, self-reliant Americans—but that is where our sinful ways have brought us and we will not see the kingdom of heaven until we face up to this reality with humble simplicity.

"Blessed are those who mourn" (Matt 5.4). Men have been brought up to believe that tears must be avoided if they are to be happy. Jesus simply says that this is not true. There is some sorrow which must be embraced, not because it is inescapable and the struggle futile, but because true happiness is impossible without it.

Even grief that is unavoidable to mortal men whatever their station can have salutary effects on our lives if we allow it to. It can, as Solomon says, remind us of the wispy momentariness of our lives and set us to thinking seriously about the most important things (Ecc 7.2–4). The psalmist who gave us such a rich meditation on the greatness of God's law has linked pain and understanding. "Before I was afflicted," he reflected, "I went astray, but now I keep Your word." He then concludes, "It is good for me that I have been afflicted, that I may learn Your statutes" (Psa 119.67, 71). Tears have always taught us more than has laughter about life's verities.

But there is something more to the mourning in this gem-like paradox than the tears we cannot escape, the sorrow that comes unbidden and unsought. This grief comes to us by choice, not necessity. The Old Testament should influence our understanding of these words first spoken to a Jewish audience. Isaiah foresaw that the Lord's anointed would come to "heal the brokenhearted" and "comfort all who mourn" (Isa 61.1–2). But these words applied only to a remnant of Israel which would come through the nation's affliction for its sins, humbled and grieved. Ezekiel's vision of God's wrath on a corrupt Jerusalem revealed that only those "who sigh and cry over all the abominations that are done within it" were to be spared (Ezek 9.4). Zephaniah issued a similar warning (Zeph 3.11–13, 18).

The prophets would have us understand this mourning as the grief experienced by those who in their reverence for God are horrified by their own sins and those of their fellows, and are moved to tears of bitter shame and grief. This is the "godly sorrow" of which Paul writes, a sorrow that "produces repentance leading to salvation" (2 Cor 7.10). These are the tears we must choose to shed, renouncing our stubborn pride; and out of that choice will come the unspeakable comfort of a God who forgives us all, takes us to Himself, and will ultimately wipe all tears away (Rev 21.4). Nothing save God's mercy can assuage a grief like this.

Beatitudes: A Gospel for Losers

"We become forgetful," writes Malcolm Muggeridge, "that Jesus is the prophet of the losers', not the victors' camp, the one who proclaims that the first will be last, that the weak are the strong and the fools are the wise" (*The End of Christendom*, p 56). Nowhere is this fact more evident than in the beatitudes. As we have already noted in our preceding study, emptiness, not fullness, is the key to happiness.

Profound Hunger

"Blessed are those who hunger and thirst for righteousness" (Matt 5.6). The word "hunger" in this beatitude is the same as that used by Matthew in the preceding chapter (Matt 4.2) when speaking of Jesus' 40-day fast in the wilderness. Since such desperate hunger is largely foreign to our experience, much in this metaphor may be lost on us. It speaks of profound spiritual starvation which is leading to death. But the parallel is not absolute. There is a fundamental difference between being stomach-hungry and heart-hungry. Even the most insensitive people are moved by the hunger of the body, yet there seem to be few who recognize the hunger of the spirit and the void that sin produces. Spiritually speaking, men resemble the half-dead corpses of Dachau and Belsen, but they stubbornly refuse to acknowledge the haunting meaninglessness of life without God. Not all those in the "far country" have the sanity to confess, like the prodigal, that they "perish with hunger" (Luke 15.17)! Such individuals continue to search mindlessly for some better "husk" to fill the emptiness. Those who "hunger and thirst for righteousness" have chosen to face their desperate need for what it is, and to seek the food that answers to it.

The "righteousness" these displaced and sin-burdened souls seek is first of all the righteousness of a right relationship with God through forgiveness and justification (Rom 5.1–2; 2 Cor

5.20–21), and, second, the concrete righteousness of a transformed life (Rom 6.8; 8.29). They not only want to feel right but
to do right. Both these ideas of righteousness are present in the
sermon (Matt 5.7 and 5.10, 20–48; 6.1). God is determined not
only to forgive us but to change us, to make us partakers of the
divine nature (2 Pet 1.4). And He has assured us that we are going
to be like Him (Matt 5.48). What a wonderful hope!

There is in every human being a built-in and inescapable need
for God. This God-hunger is movingly expressed by David while
a fugitive from Saul: "My soul thirsts for You; my flesh longs for
You in a dry and weary land where there is no water" (Psa 63.1).
Sin has put in every man a God-shaped emptiness. Characteristi-
cally, we try to ease our pain by pouring in all kinds of unbelievable trash. But we had as well try to pour Niagara Falls into a tea-
cup as to seek to satisfy our God-akin spirits with mere "things"
and carnal thrills. Unable to meet our fundamental need, money
and pleasure and even worldly wisdom become the basis for an
insatiable appetite that leaves us empty, unfulfilled and burnt out
(Ecc 5.10–11). We will never be able to have enough, feel enough,
or know enough, to find contentment without God. What we
need is righteousness and, as Jesus says, those that long for it are
destined to know a transcendent satisfaction and peace—**"they
shall be filled"** (Matt 5.6).

There is in this beatitude a call for a change of priorities. For
many of us a right relationship with God is seen as an important part of "the good life" which every well-rounded individual
should address, but it is certainly not the whole of things. Jesus
says that it must be more than a vital interest—it must become
the reigning passion of our existence. All that truly hungry people
can think of is food.

"Blessed are the pure in heart" (Matt 5.8). J. B. Phillips translates this phrase, "Blessed are the utterly sincere," and this would
appear to reflect the true meaning of our Lord's words. The purity
in this beatitude certainly does not refer to perfect righteousness
of life, and given the fact that attitudes (things we must have as

opposed to what God does) dominate this part of the sermon, it is unlikely that it refers principally to the purity of a forgiven heart. It is far more probable that it speaks of the purity of a single-minded devotion (Matt 6.22–24; 2 Cor 11.2), an attitude which is possible even for sinners (Luke 8.15). James makes this use of purity when he urges: "Draw near to God and He will draw near to you. Cleanse your hands, you sinners; and purify your hearts, you double-minded" (Jas 4.8). The true vision of God will not be granted to the shrewd and calculating who play dishonest games, or to the double-minded who can never quite put both feet in the kingdom (Jas 1.7–8), but to those who are absolutely honest and single of heart toward God. They will see God (Matt 5.8), not as the Jews at Sinai, but in the full understanding of an intimate relationship with Him (John 3.3–5; 14.7–9). It is an old question with an old answer. "Who," says David, "may ascend into the hill of the LORD ... or ... stand in His holy place? He who has clean hands and a pure heart" (Psa 24.3–4). If you want to see God with your whole heart, you will. People like that don't let *any-thing* stand in their way.

Beatitudes: *Matt 5: 3 - 10*
The Strength of "Weakness"

The second basic statement of the beatitudes is that the kingdom of God does not yield itself to the "mighty" who seek to take it by force, but it is easily accessible to the "weak" who yield their cause patiently to God and abandon their own rights for the sake of others. The world in which the beatitudes were first spoken was not a hospitable place for such an idea. Seneca, a prominent first-century stoic philosopher and brother of Gallio (Acts 18.12), gave expression to the sentiment of his times in the following words: "Pity is a mental illness induced by the spectacle of other people's miseries. ...The sage does not succumb to mental diseases of that sort" (Arnold Toynbee, *An Historian's Approach to Religion,* p 68). Wholly outside the spirit of His age, Jesus announced the blessedness of the meek, the merciful, the peacemakers and the persecuted. It was not an idea "whose time had come." It still is not.

"Blessed are the meek" (Matt 5.5, KJV). In a world of harshness and cruelty, meekness would appear to be a quick way to commit suicide. The violent and self-willed prevail. The meek are summarily run over. The truth is that in the short run this may indeed be so. People that are drawn to the kingdom of God must face this. The gentleness of Jesus did not save Him from the cross. But, ultimately, Jesus teaches us, it is meekness alone that will survive. The challenge for us is to understand what true meekness is.

Meekness is not a natural disposition. It is not an inborn mildness of temperament. It is not the obsequious behavior of a slave whose powerless station forces him to adopt a servile manner which he despises and would abandon at the first opportunity. Meekness is an attitude toward God and others which is the product of choice. It is a disposition held by a steely moral resolve at a time when one may have the power, and the inclination, to behave otherwise.

Meekness is not an indifference to evil. Jesus endured with much patience the assaults made on Him, but He was strong to defend His Father's name and will. He hated iniquity as much as He loved righteousness (Heb 1.9). Moses was the meekest of men when it came to abuse offered to him (Num 12.3), but his anger could burn hot against irreverence offered to God (Exod 32.19). The meek man may endure mistreatment patiently (he is not concerned with *self*-defense) but he is not passive about evil (Rom 12.9). There is in him a burning hatred for every false way (Gal 1.8–9; Psa 119.104).

Meekness is not weakness. There is no flabbiness in it. The one who had 72,000 angels at His command (Matt 26.53) described Himself as "gentle and lowly in heart" (Matt 11.29). The depth of meekness in a man may indeed be gauged in direct proportion to his ability to crush his adversaries. Jesus was not meek because He was powerless. He was meek because He had His immense power under the control of great principles—His love for His Father (John 14.31) and His love for lost men (Eph 5.2). It would have been far easier for Him to have simply annihilated His foes than to patiently endure their abuse. He took the hard road.

The meekness of the Son of God is powerfully demonstrated in His attitude toward the privileges of His station ("who, existing in the form of God, counted not the being on an equality with God a thing to be grasped, but emptied himself," Phil 2.6–7 ASV), and in His submission to His Father ("though He was a Son, yet He learned obedience by the things which He suffered," Heb 5.8). He came into the world as a servant. He emptied Himself for the sake of others.

Although kingdom meekness derives from a new view of oneself in the presence of God ("poor in spirit") its primary emphasis is on a man's view of himself in the presence of others. "Meekness" (Greek, *praus)* is found in the constant company of words like "lowliness," "kindness," "longsuffering," "forbearance," and "gentleness"

(Eph 4.2; Col 3.12–13; 2 Tim 2.24–25; Tit 3.2; 2 Cor 10.1). Even when applied to our Savior the word seems to speak to His relationship to men rather than to His Father (Matt 11.28–30; 2 Cor 10.1). "Meekness" *(praus)* had a special use in the ancient Greek world. It was applied to an animal that had been tamed (Barclay, *New Testament Words,* p 241). The meek man is one who has been tamed to the yoke of Christ (Matt 11.29) and, consequently, has taken up the burdens of other men (Gal 6.2). He no longer seeks to take by force even that which is rightfully his nor attempts to avenge the injustices done him—not because he is powerless to do so, but because he has submitted his cause to a higher court (Rom 12.19). Instead he is concerned to be a blessing, not only to his brethren (Rom 15.3), but even to his enemies (Luke 6.27–28).

The meek man has had enough of himself. He has felt his own ultimate spiritual emptiness and yearned for a right relationship with God. *Self*-righteousness has become a disaster and *self*-will a sickness. The very ideas of *self*-confidence and *self*-assertiveness have become a stench in his nostrils. He has emptied his heart of self and filled it with God and others. Like his Master, he has become the ultimate servant. And for this very reason the future belongs to him.

Beatitudes: A Surprising Conclusion

With this article we bring to a conclusion our study of the beatitudes. They end as they began, in a startling way.

"Blessed are the merciful" (Matt 5.7). Mercy is a quality not wholly unknown even in a world of basically self-seeking men. But it is a selective, capricious mercy that does not move from principle and is not a settled disposition of the heart and character. The same man who is capable of occasional compassion still finds the sorrows of others too burdensome and revenge too sweet.

The mercy which Jesus praises is borne of the penetrating awareness of one's own desperate need of mercy, not simply from men, but specially from God. It is mercy that shows compassion to the helpless (Luke 10.37) and extends forgiveness even to the one who gives repeated offense (Matt 18.21–22). This compassion is not prompted by the appealing qualities of the offender (How would we treat the "ugly" sinner?) but rises from our own sense of gratitude for that mercy which God has shown *us*. We also were not appealing when God sent His Son to the cross (Rom 5.8). Citizens of heaven's commonwealth have not forgotten which side of the tracks they came from (Tit 3.1–5). One of the greatest expressions of this kind of mercy is its selfless concern for a sinful and unattractive but lost world (Matt 9.36–38). It is a driving force in gospel preaching.

Mercy toward men does not *merit* mercy from God, but it is an evidence of the penitent spirit which is a divine condition of forgiveness (Matt 18.23–35). Kingdom citizens live among their fellows, not as an arrogant spiritual aristocracy, but as forgiven, and forgiving men.

"Blessed are the peacemakers" (Matt 5.9). This beatitude is not without its challenges. Men are tempted to apply it to those irenic spirits whose gift for negotiation and compromise pours oil on troubled waters. But the whole context of the sermon rebels against this view. These are not peacemakers in the ordinary sense of mediating human disputes, but in the ultimate sense of bringing to men the peace of Christ (John 14.27). What is the value of peace bought at the price of principle or of a momentary tranquility that is not grounded on reconciliation with God? The true peacemakers are those who are themselves at peace with God (Rom 5.1) and men (Rom 12.18) and who preach in the world a gospel of peace and reconciliation (Eph 2.13–17). No other people could be called the children of "the God of peace" (Rom 15.33). When men are reconciled to God and the peace of Christ rules in their hearts, the spirit of compassion, meekness and forgiveness produced in them ministers reconciliation with all men (Col 3.12–15). If, in spite of all, others are still disposed to see such people as enemies, the fault does not lie in them. They are the true servants of peace in the world.

"Blessed are those who are persecuted for righteousness' sake" (Matt 5.10–12). Here is a concluding surprise. These peacemakers have become the persecuted! Jesus, having now dealt with the attitude of kingdom citizens toward God, themselves, and others, now turns to consider the attitude of the world toward them. One would have thought that such people as Jesus has described would be received with great rejoicing in the world—a humble people, heedless of themselves, given to the needs of others. To the contrary, the Lord now reveals that they will stir the world to a bitter animosity and hatred.

The Son of God has never sought to withhold the realities of suffering from His followers. His candor with those who enthusiastically sought Him is remarkable. He urged them even in their ardor to soberly count the cost (Matt 8.19–20; Luke 14.26–33). The Lord will have no disciples out of their naiveté. He wants no sudden shocks to destroy their faith. He has spoken plainly so that when His disciples suffer they can know that it is just as He said it would be and take heart with the assurance that their Master's promises of glory are just as sure—"for He who promised is faithful" (Heb 10.23).

And what is the cause of this hateful, knowing persecution of a humble, gentle people? Not some secret malignant conspiracy. Not the clandestine practice of unholy and immoral rites. Their crime is simple. They have chosen to be righteous in an unrighteous world. They are too much like their Master (John 15.18–20). Their love and simplicity only serve to throw into harsher relief the dark selfishness of an ungodly generation which hates the light and feels keenly the silent judgment of the Christians' contrasting innocence (John 3.19–20).

The Lord's disciples should rejoice at an opposition which reveals that the spirit and character of their Savior has been seen in them. They should rejoice because they have been granted the privilege of suffering for one who endured such abuse for their sakes (Phil 1.28–29; Acts 5.41). But, most of all, they should rejoice because their suffering is not empty. They can embrace it joyfully, knowing that it transforms the character (Jas 1.2–4) and works for them "a far more exceeding and eternal weight of glory" (2 Cor 4.17). No temporal threat can intimidate the one whose true treasure is secured in heaven. As one has observed: "He is no fool who gives what he cannot keep to gain what he cannot lose."

Similitudes:
The Calling of the Christian

With every beatitude the gulf between kingdom citizens and the world of ordinary men has widened. Jesus has clearly issued a call for His disciples to make a moral and spiritual exit from a society ruled by pride and passion. This separation to a new life was to be conclusively sealed by the world's own bitter reaction. They are to be slandered, assaulted and rejected. Their gentle and humble ways would never suffice to allay the sense of embarrassment, intimidation and fear which their righteous ways were destined to evoke. The break was to be complete.

And yet, ironically enough, the very people who have become, in effect, the off-scouring of the earth are, in reality, the world's only hope. As the beatitudes have delineated the character of citizens of the heavenly commonwealth, so now the similitudes (Matt 5.13–16) make clear their calling. Though set apart to God and separated distinctly from the society of other men, they are nevertheless related to the world in a very special way.

Time has somewhat dispelled the apparent absurdity of this scene on a Galilean hillside. Jesus is telling this nondescript knot of men and women that they were marked out to preserve and illuminate the world. They had little money, no worldly standing, and no prospects. Some "wise" heads must have been no little amused by all this pompous talk. Visionaries had arisen before in the nation, created a momentary excitement, and then evaporated (Acts 5.35–37). The poor prospects of this movement made even the hopeless visions of a Theudas or a Judas of Galilee seem positively promising.

Nevertheless time was to reveal an amazing eventuality. The things that looked so durable in those days vanished. The Roman

Empire collapsed. Plato's academy closed. The schools of the Stoics and Epicureans faded to a curiosity. The great library at Alexandria burned. But the company of the Christians endured. They would still possess no great wealth or worldly standing, but their message would be very much alive and their spirit vital. Lives would be changed everywhere.

It should not surprise us that the One who came to save a lost humanity (Luke 19.10) should draw all His disciples into that great enterprise. His task was to become their task; His passion their passion.

"You are the salt of the earth" (Matt 5.13). **"You are the light of the world"** (Matt 5.14). The metaphors Jesus chose to illustrate the critical nature of the kingdom's calling were fashioned out of common household materials. Not a house in Palestine was without some salt, or a lamp to chase away the evening gloom. The world of men, because of sin, was putrefying in the darkness. Citizens of heaven's kingdom were destined to be the salt to stay sin's rot and the light to penetrate its dark despair. Still Jesus warned His disciples that the world they intended to preserve, they might also lose.

The kingdom of heaven was not intended to turn inward upon itself, like some giant monastery. Its citizens were not intended to live in grand isolation. Though not *of* the world they were to be very much *in* the world (John 17.14–15). Their Master was always a man of the people. His life was lived amidst the thronging multitudes of Palestine. He was always accessible, always vulnerable, always concerned. He spent His time among the troubled and distressed (Luke 15.1–2). This is something Christians must never forget. We may be persecuted, as He was (John 15.19–20), but we must never allow our pain to dry up our compassion. We may be weary at times, as He was (John 4.6), but we can never permit our weariness to turn us away from the needs of others. The kingdom from above may indeed be a citadel against sin but it is always to be the refuge for the sinner.

"If the salt loses its flavor" (Matt 5.13). Kingdom citizens, though very much in the world, must never become worldly. The salt must not lose its saltiness (Luke 14.34–35; Mark 9.50). Their savor rests in the holy distinctiveness of their lives and character. The passion for righteousness must never be compromised or the disciple's usefulness is at an end. Though salt in fact cannot cease to be salty, it can, like the salty powder that forms on the shores of the Dead Sea, become so polluted that it is as useless as road dust. If by concessions made to the world the salt has been leached out of us, leaving only a residue of worldly respectability, fine buildings, congenial social circles and empty rituals, we, too, have become utterly worthless!

One final thought. As important as it is for Christians to worship God according to His will, we must remember that most lost men will not be made to glorify God because we eat the Lord's supper every Sunday. They may indeed be moved to exalt God by the quiet love with which we bear one another (John 13.34–35), by our self-control in the face of great provocation, by our calm assurance in the presence of tragedy, and our firm refusal to be drawn into a world of mindless lusts. If we have gained the victory over a worldly system of pride and carnality (1 John 2.15–17; 5.4) it will surely show, and God, not ourselves, will be glorified.

The Righteousness of the Kingdom: Jesus and the Law

We have now come to the heart of Jesus' great address. The beatitudes have outlined the special spiritual character of the kingdom citizen. The similitudes have dealt with the kingdom's high and noble calling. Now Jesus addresses Himself to the quality of kingdom righteousness. His treatment is specific and to the point and essentially continues from Matthew 5.17 until He begins His final appeal in Matthew 7.13.

"I came not to destroy the law ... but to fulfill" (Matt 5.17–18, KJV). Jesus prefaces His discussion of kingdom righteousness with a powerful disclaimer. He has not come, He says emphatically, to destroy the law and the prophets. Why was such a disavowal necessary? Did He not claim to be the Christ of prophetic promise? Yes, but sometimes appearances overwhelm words. A brief look at the events which preceded the delivery of this discourse will provide an answer to our question.

The Pharisees, as a party, represented the most dedicated defenders of the law in the nation of Israel. While the Sadducees busied themselves with Temple politics, the Pharisees studied and taught the law as viewed in the traditions of their fathers. In the mind of many in the Jewish community the law of Moses and the traditions of the Pharisees were identical. It would have been the cause of no little anxiety among the people to see Jesus come head to head continuously with these established teachers of the national covenant.

The Pharisees were greatly displeased with the company Jesus kept (Mark 2.16–17; Luke 5.30–32), and by the time Jesus preached His great sermon on the kingdom He had had at least three bitter confrontations with the Pharisees over Sabbath observance (Luke 6.1–11; Mark 2.23–3.6; John 5.2–18). The disagreement was now so deep that the Pharisees had already determined to destroy Him (Mark 3.6; Luke 6.11).

This sharp conflict with the known party of the law must have convinced many that Jesus intended to destroy the law and build again on its ruins. The Pharisees would not have been slow to exploit such an impression. The Lord is now, therefore, at considerable pains to explode this misconception. It would soon become apparent in His sermon that His conflict was not with the law but with the Pharisaic perversions of it.

Jesus' attitude toward the Old Testament Scriptures now becomes unmistakably clear. Because they are His Father's words, far from being abolished or subverted, they are to be fulfilled to the last minute detail, and, even more significantly, *He* was to fulfill them! Three great truths surface here. Jesus ties Himself inseparably to the God of the Old Testament. The God of Abraham, Isaac and Jacob is also the God and Father of our Lord Jesus Christ. Jesus also confirms His absolute confidence in the integrity of every word of the Old Testament writings. They are the words of God, and anyone who would be His disciple must have the same high view of Scripture (Luke 24.25–27; John 10.35). And then there emerges for the first time in the sermon the awesome greatness of the preacher. He is to be the fulfillment of God's eternal purpose, the consummation of the ages, the end point of all history. This is no mere ethical treatise. The sermon is great, but the preacher is greater still.

What does Jesus mean when He speaks of fulfilling the law and the prophets? He is certainly not speaking of binding upon kingdom citizens every last precept of the Mosaic covenant which by rabbinic count numbered 613! No one to our knowledge holds this view. Paul was later to state clearly that these ordinances about food and feasts and Sabbaths had nothing to do with serving Christ but were fulfilled in His death and removed (Col 2.14–17).

Does the Lord then refer to His own perfect obedience to the law? Jesus, who was born under the law (Gal 4.4), did indeed observe the law's command with flawless perfection (1 Pet 2.22), yet

His concern here is *fulfillment* of purpose, not *observation* of precept. Jesus was destined to be the fulfillment of all the Old Testament types and shadows (Col 2.17; Heb 10.1–4) and the realization of all Old Testament prophecies (Luke 24.25–27, 44–48). He was to be the culmination of the law's purpose to lead men to justification through faith in Him (Gal 3.24–25; Rom 10.4). Having done its work, the law was ended, and led, as it had always promised, to the establishment of a new covenant with better promises (Jer 31.31–34; Heb 8.6–8). The citizen of the kingdom is under law to Christ (1 Cor 9.21) and in the fullness of Christ he is made full (Col 2.9–10). All efforts to turn from Christ back to the law are a case of arrested spiritual development.

But having said all that, it must be remembered that the ethical teachings of Jesus do not represent a radical departure from the law, but are a natural extension of the two greatest commandments which are first found in the law: "You shall love the LORD your God with all your heart" (Deut 6.5) and "You shall love your neighbor as yourself" (Lev 19.18). The great difference between the law and the gospel is not to be found in their respective ethical demands but in the sacrificial death of the Son of God.

The Kingdom and God's Commandments

"**Whoever therefore breaks one of the least of these command-ments...**" (Matt 5.19). Jesus, having cut the ground from under any notion that He came to destroy the law and the prophets by promising their complete fulfillment (Matt 5.17–18), now extends His point by addressing the issue of the kingdom's relationship to the commandments of God.

One is tempted to think that Jesus is dealing here (Matt 5.19) with some heady libertines who may have imagined, happily, that Jesus' troubles with the establishment rabbis meant that He intended to free men from the burdensome task of keeping God's law. The context, however, points to the Pharisees as the culprits (Matt 5.20). The people primarily under the gun are not those who in weakness violate a divine command, but teachers of the law who go beyond personal transgression to breaking the very authority of the commands. This is a perfect picture of the Pharisees who by their traditions had subverted the law of God (Mark 7.1–13).

Still, though Jesus may have legalists more than libertines in mind here, His statement has valid application to those "free" spirits who see in the gospel an end to all law. Not only does this fly in the face of the testimony of Scripture (1 Cor 9.21; Gal 6.2; Jas 1.25), but it has implications of the most serious kind. Without law sin cannot exist (1 John 3.4) and without sin grace becomes unnecessary and meaningless (1 John 1.7, 9).

It would be exceedingly helpful if students of the Scripture could realize that God's law or will for man inheres in creation, not in the covenants. The Creator's expectations for His creature, man, have been in place since Adam. The two greatest commandments (Deut 6.5; Lev 19.18; Mark 12.28–31) did not first have application when they were included in the covenant made with Israel at Sinai, but were clearly applied to man's behavior toward God and others from his inception (Gen 4.1–12; 6.5, 11–13; 18.20; Jude 7). A man is not under law to God because he is under covenant (new or old). He is under law to God because he is a man. One can only escape God's law by resigning from the human race. Resignations have frequently been tendered, but there is no evidence that any have been accepted. Man, under covenant, makes a commitment to be faithful to God and His commands and receives in turn the promises and blessings of the Lord—but whatever he does there is no escape from divine law.

But why, it is asked, does Jesus, in a sermon on the "gospel of the kingdom," urge upon His hearers the careful keeping of the least commandment of the law of Moses? The answer is: because His audience was Jewish and were, even as Jesus spoke, under that covenant. Whatever attitude they had toward God's law as expressed in the Jewish covenant they were bound to bring to the kingdom. The covenant is not so important as the principle of absolute trust and obedience toward God in everything. Anyone disposed to play fast and loose with the smallest command of God, whatever the covenant, is unfit for the kingdom of heaven. A new covenant would come but the principle would remain the same.

Some ordinances of God are manifestly greater than others because they sit closer to the heart of divine righteousness (Mark 12.28–33; Matt 23.23), but no command of God is without immense significance since the breath of the Almighty is in it (2 Tim 3.16). The one who rebuked the Pharisees for swallowing camels did not encourage them to eat gnats with relish (Matt 23.23). James has sought to make us understand that the commands of God are indivisible since *He* is behind them all (Jas 2.10–11). It is not just a matter of breaking a command, little or great. It is a matter of defying God and breaking faith with Him.

Obedience is not limited as a principle to systems of justification by law (Gal 3.10). It is also an expression of faith (Jas 2.14–26) and love (John 14.15, 23–24; 1 John 5.3) in the gospel system of grace and justification by faith (Matt 7.21). As such it has application to salvation in every dispensation (Heb 11). The kingdom citizen, like the faithful of all ages, is not seeking to justify *himself* by his earnest obedience to all God's commands, but to return the love which has been poured out upon him so undeservedly. The law of God is a dagger to the heart of the arrogant and self-righteous, but to the Christian it is the standard of righteous conduct to which, under the grace of God, he aspires (Rom 12.1–2). God intends not only to redeem His people but to transform them as well (Rom 8.29; 2 Cor 3.18).

"...shall be called least in the kingdom of heaven" (Matt 5.19b). Many otherwise responsible commentators have sought to deprive Jesus' warning of its force by suggesting that those who treat lightly God's lesser commands will not suffer any serious loss. Admitted to heaven's stadium they will simply have to sit in the bleachers rather than in the box seats! We strongly dissent from this view because (1) the rest of the sermon does not agree with it (Matt 7.21, 24–27), and (2) the expression "great" or "greatest in the kingdom" is used by Jesus elsewhere in Matthew to refer to every citizen in the kingdom (Matt 18.1–4; 20.26–28), admitting of no place for "the least."

Beware of those teachers who think they know which of God's commandments are important and which are not!

A Different Kind of Righteousness

"Unless your righteousness exceeds the righteousness of the scribes and Pharisees, you will by no means enter the kingdom of heaven" (Matt 5.20). Jesus has opened the body of His sermon on the nature of the kingdom righteousness by making two clear statements. The first is that He came to fulfill, rather than to destroy, the law and the prophets and to demand reverence for every command of God (Matt 5.17–19). The second is that He came to make war on the "righteousness" of the Pharisees. His quarrel was not with God's word. It never had been. But the corruptions of the establishment hypocrites had shut the door of the kingdom against the people (Matt 23.13). Jesus knew that if ever the nation was to understand the true righteousness of God the Pharisaic distortions of God's law had to be blasted away. The view of the Pharisees notwithstanding, the great threat to the divine kingdom did not come from Gentile impurity but from their own grotesque mutilations of the very law they proudly boasted of protecting. Here Jesus denounces their wholly inadequate system of righteousness by name, and warns that it will never suffice to see a man into the kingdom of heaven (Matt 5.20).

In this very irenic age, which treasures peace and harmony even above truth and righteousness, the plain language of the Savior will make many uncomfortable. The Son of God was never cute or needlessly severe in His treatment of false teachers but He did not hesitate to "call names" when it was necessary to identify the well from which His people were being poisoned. It needs to be remembered today that Jesus attacked the religious establishment, not out of personal vanity and ambition, but because the souls of men He loved hung in the balance. We would do well to imitate Him. We must be prudent and fair but we must speak plainly when the salvation of lost men requires it.

The "righteousness" of the Pharisees was a particular way of looking at things which would always have been inadequate in the kingdom of God even if served up by the carloads. It was not the quantity which fell short but the quality. It was the wrong *kind* of righteousness.

It is possible that the Pharisees had not always been what they had become in Jesus' day. Even then there were Pharisees of deep integrity like Saul of Tarsus. Their ancestors, unable to keep inviolate the holy city, were determined to preserve from Gentile pollution the holy law. This strict party of separatists likely had their origin at some time during the second or third centuries BC when Greek thought was threatening to engulf the Jews. But the resistance which began so nobly was soon reduced to an accentuated formalism without spiritual depth (Matt 23.27–28), and their sense of separation from the world turned to an arrogant self-righteousness (Luke 18.9–14). The movement that had begun in order to bring glory to God was now dedicated to the exaltation of a smug, sanctimonious elite which had interest only in itself. And, most ironic, the effort to protect the sanctity of the law had resulted in its corruption by endless scribal traditions (Mark 7.8–9).

The Pharisees were in a superb position to know the law and could have been brought to the humble service of God by an awareness of its full demand. From such a position of honesty they would have felt an increasing sense of the need of God's help to attain to righteousness. Instead, rather than face their own inadequacy, they simply chopped the law and the prophets down to the measure of their own moral and spiritual dwarfism. The law was now reduced in their hands to little more than mindless rituals possessed of justifying merit and its spiritual heart was cut out by turning its profound moral precepts into a superficial civil law. Above all, it no longer had any connection with love. The kingdom of God had no place for this hypocritical, self-righteous configuration of human traditions which Pharisaism had become (Matt 15.3–20). The righteousness of the kingdom from above is one of the heart—a righteousness that begins at the fountainhead of thought and will and issues in deeds and words (Luke 6.43–45).

As the succeeding verses will reveal, the righteousness about which Jesus now speaks is primarily a righteousness of life and conduct—the transformed life of the kingdom citizen. There is no teaching here of justification by works. This kind of transformation comes only to the poor in spirit who know only too well their need for God's mercy, but it is a transformation that is necessary. If we are to succeed in the kingdom life we must do our Father's will (Matt 5.19; 7.21, 24–28) and grow up into His perfect love (Matt 5.44–48).

The True Righteousness

"**You have heard ... but I say to you**" (Matt 5.21–22). With this oft-repeated contrast beating a heavy cadence Jesus opens the heart of His discourse on true righteousness. But it was not a sermon preached in a vacuum. The problem of Pharisaic righteousness has been openly raised and now this baneful system will be methodically cut to pieces by the Lord's penetrating and authoritative observations. It was not too much devotion to the law which elicited Jesus' devastating attack on the Pharisees, but too little. With arrogant hypocrisy they had produced an empty parody of God's law. Jesus rejects their sham and exposes it for what it is in the light of the true and unchanging righteousness of God.

If, as some suppose, Jesus was here quoting the Old Testament Scriptures He uses a different approach than at any other time. On no other occasion did He ever introduce Scripture with, "You have heard that it was said to those of old." Earlier, when tempted by Satan in the wilderness, Jesus introduced three passages from Deuteronomy with the words, "It is written" (Matt 4.5, 7, 10). He used the same form in Matthew 11.10 and 21.13. In other instances the Lord indicated the writer from which He was quoting (Matt 12.17; 13.14, 35; 15.7; 21.4; 22.43) or simply cited "the Scriptures" (Matt 21.42). The different treatment in Matthew 5.21–48 is too marked to be ignored. Here Jesus is citing, not the Scripture, but "the tradition of the elders" (Mark 7.5).

The context of this part of the Lord's sermon points in the same direction. Jesus has just made a point of expressing His reverence for the law and the prophets (Matt 5.17–19). Is it reasonable to think that He would then turn and unleash a withering attack on that very law? The immediate concern of the preacher as He begins this section of His address is the sham righteousness of the Pharisees (Matt 5.20) and this is the problem with which He deals in the succeeding verses (Matt 5.21–48).

The contrast being drawn in these verses is not between the law of Moses and the law of Christ. It is rather a contrast between the Pharisaic corruptions of the Old Testament and the true righteousness of the kingdom—a righteousness that was anticipated in the law and brought to its fullness in Christ. As we have earlier observed, the ethical teachings of Jesus do not represent a radical departure form the Old Testament ethics. The foundation commands of the law—to love God supremely and one's neighbor as oneself (Deut 6.5; Lev 19.18)—are taken by the Lord as the bulwark of His own teachings (Matt 7.12; 22.34–40). The ethical principles of the Old Testament were not superficial ordinances which governed muscle but not mind. The tenth commandment of the Decalogue addresses itself directly to the mind and heart (Exod 20.17). And who could read this ancient Jewish covenant and imagine that the God who spoke from Sinai would allow His people to hate as long as they did not kill, or lust as long as it was not consummated? It was He who said, "You shall not hate your brother in your heart" (Lev 19.17) and, "You shall not covet your neighbor's wife" (Deut 5.21).

The law of Moses, in its essence, reflected God's true ethical demands. While it is true that the law made concessions to Israel's "hardness of heart" (Matt 19.8; Mark 10.5) and contained many "fleshly ordinances" (Heb 9.10), yet at its heart, as Paul affirmed, "the law is spiritual" (Rom 7.14) "and the commandment holy and just and good" (Rom 7.12).

The ethical demands of the Sermon on the Mount are simply the flower that issued from the Old Testament bud. While it is true that grace and the fullness of truth came by Jesus Christ (John 1.17), it is also true that there was ethical and spiritual truth in the law and a clear anticipation of the grace to come (Gal 3.8).

So, though it is accurate to say that Jesus is exposing Pharisaic perversions of the law, it is not accurate to say that Jesus does no more than give a correct exposition of Old Testament ethics. Jesus clearly anchors His ethical teachings in the ethics of the law, but

He does not stop there. He goes on to expand them into the law of the kingdom of heaven.

The aim of the kingdom is the righteousness of God (Matt 5.48; 6.33). In order to lead His hearers to an understanding of that moral and spiritual order of things Jesus begins with the more obvious moral imperatives of what it means to love others (Matt 5.21–48). There is an ascending plane in these verses. The Lord begins on a negative note—with the prohibition that most commends itself to men even in their lowest estate—"You shall not murder." As the chapter concludes He has risen to love's most positive and demanding thrust—not love as men know it, but love as God in His holy perfection demonstrates it.

These verses are not comfortable to read and they are often challenging to understand, but the student must always keep in mind that beneath all these instructions is that second of the great commandments, "You shall love your neighbor as yourself." In terms both practical and to the point we are now to be confronted with what it means to be a citizen in the kingdom of heaven.

"Whoever Hates His Brother..."

This section of the sermon (Matt 5.21–48) begins with a consideration of how the kingdom citizen is to deal with his own inclination to evil, and then closes (Matt 5.38–48) with a study of how he is to meet evil in others.

There is in these passages the description of a radical kind of love. If it startles us who stand this side of the cross, what a jolt it must have given those who first heard it *before* the unthinkable events of Calvary. Though only anticipated in Jesus' summit address, it seems evident that God's radical love for men in Christ was to be the indispensable foundation for such a holy and selfless devotion to others. Like the woman whose prodigal expression of love for Jesus shocked the Lord's Pharisee host (Luke 7.36–50), we love much because we have been forgiven much. God's radical love for us releases within us a radical capacity for good will toward others. And the nature of that love, like our Lord's, is to be sacrificial (Matt 16.24–25). As Jesus emptied Himself for our sakes so must we empty ourselves for the sake of others (Phil 2.1–8).

But why all these specifics? Why not issue the simple instruction to love one's neighbor as oneself and be done with it? It is because we are all so lacking in understanding of our own best interests and, consequently, those of others. A drunkard, practicing "neighbor love," might give his fellow sot another drink of whiskey. Thomas Harris raises this problem rather left-handedly in his book, *I'm O.K., You're O.K.:* "The Golden Rule is not an adequate guide, not because the ideal is wrong, but because most people do not have enough data about what they want for themselves, or why they want it." The missing data is provided in the teachings of Christ and His apostles. Their instructions fill out the practical details of what it means to love God and to work for the real best interests of other people. This information does not arise from our own unguided wishes or judgments as Harris and situation ethics suggest, but from God's divine wisdom. It cannot be otherwise. From our very restricted human point of view we cannot possibly know all the implications of our behavior even when well intended. God informs and guides our love with His moral instruction. As John observes: "By this we know that we love the children of God, when we love God and keep His commandments" (1 John 5.2).

The Pharisees were always inclined to lower the moral and spiritual level of the law and increase the ceremonial demand. Jesus begins this section with a perfect example of Pharisaic reductionism. **"You have heard that it was said to those of old, 'You shall not murder, and whoever murders will be in danger of the judgment'"** (Matt 5.21). The troublesome thing about these citations is that they at times seem to be exact quotations of the law. "You shall not murder" is straight out of Exodus 20.13 and Deuteronomy 5.17. The "judgment" of the second citation refers to the local council or court, and although the citation is not an exact quotation of the law it accurately reflects the words of Numbers 35.30–31. And yet in the hands of the Pharisees these were not the law but ideas lifted from the law and perverted. The concern of the establishment hacks was that no one should commit an act which brought down a civil penalty. The only crimes which disturbed their conscience were those which could be treated by human tribunals. They were deeply disturbed by murder, but hatred and malice caused them no serious consternation. However abusive their ways toward others, as long as there was no blood-guiltiness they felt themselves righteous before the law.

Jesus' response (Matt 5.22) accommodates itself to their fixation with civil penalties. The truth is, He says, that the man who harbors a loveless anger against his brother is in danger of the local court. John later reflected this concept in his memorable statement, "Whoever hates his brother is a murderer" (1 John 3.15).

Having addressed the problem of the heart Jesus extends His application to the tongue. Not only do bitter feelings put one in jeopardy but so also does the contemptuous abuse they are disposed to foster. How many hearts have been brutalized by words that cut like rapiers. At times murder would be more humane than these verbal atrocities! We lash out at people in utter scorn and leave them, as we intended, broken. For this, the Lord warned, you will be "in danger of the council" (a likely reference to the Sanhedrin) or, more to the point, "hell fire." It is evident that the Lord's use of "judgment" and "council" here are accommodative. Civil courts cannot deal with wicked thoughts, but the tribunal to which Jesus refers can cast the offender into hell (Matt 10.28).

Our youthful reaction to this teaching disposed us to call a man anything but sensible, but to avoid calling him a "fool" at all costs. ("Raca" gave us no problem since we didn't know what it meant anyway.) The Pharisees would have loved this interpretation!

The problem of murder must be dealt with at the fountain-head—both heart and tongue, as well as hand, must be cleansed of hatred's brutality. The law taught this (Lev 19.17) but the Pharisees in their great sweat to obtain cheap righteousness managed to overlook it. The Lord does not intend that we shall.

Dealing with Your Victim

"First be reconciled to your brother" (Matt 5.24). Jesus began this section of His sermon with a series of warnings about the severe judgment destined to fall upon those who allow their anger to issue in hateful verbal abuse of others. He continues His theme by outlining the only way of escape for such offenders of the law of neighbor love (Matt 5.23–26).

What Jesus requires of us when we sin in this way is what the majority of men seem to dread most intensely: He demands that we face and deal with our victim. The context indicates that the brother who "has something against you" is not just someone who is disgruntled, but one whom we have indeed wronged. In this case the worshiper is guilty, not just misunderstood. Other verses confirm this meaning (Mark 11.25). The gift-offerer needs to repent and seek his wronged brother's forgiveness. The dispatch with which the guilty party is to act, breaking off right in the midst of sacrifice, reflects the urgency of the situation and emphasizes how the mistreatment of others negates the worship of God. Scripture is full of this principle (Psa 66.18; Jas 3.9–10; 1 John 4.20–21). The abuse of others serves to shut the door of heaven against us.

While the secularist has tended to treat worship with a measure of contempt as he emphasizes right conduct toward others, many religionists have historically tried to use worship as a cover for moral failure. This was the long suit of the Pharisees who sought to expiate by zealous ceremony their abuse of men (Matt 23.23–24). But the Pharisee did not originate this skewed view of things. Several centuries earlier Amos had warned the smug citizens of Samaria that God had had His fill of their pretentious worship. What the Lord wanted, said the farmer-prophet, was righteousness and justice (Amos 5.21–24). Jeremiah, a hundred years later, had echoed the same theme in Jerusalem (Jer 7.21–23). Jesus tried to teach the Pharisees the lesson of the prophets. He sent them more than once to the words of Hosea: "I desire mercy and not sacrifice" (Matt 9.13; 12,7). The Lord had little success in His endeavor but there were always the few like the scribe who observed that to love God with all the heart and one's neighbor as oneself was "more than all the whole burnt offerings and sacrifices" (Mark 12,32–33). Jesus said that he was not far from the kingdom.

So what is the lesson here? When we have sinned against another the need is not for more dedicated attendance at worship assemblies or greater liberality in the Sunday collections or more spirited personal evangelism, though these generally might be more seriously treated by all of us. The urgent need of the hour is for repentance and reconciliation with our injured brother or sister. (Husbands and wives especially need to hear this. Remember that husbands and wives and children are "neighbors," too). David addressed himself to this matter in the case of his own grievous moral failure with Bathsheba and Uriah: "For You do not desire sacrifice, or else I would give it; You do not delight in burnt offering. The sacrifices of God are a broken spirit, a broken and a contrite heart—these, O God, You will not despise" (Psa 51.16–17). Don't try to offer God worship when repentance is required.

We must learn to address our sin and those we sin against with directness. "I have wronged you; please forgive me" are words that have gotten no easier to say with the passing years, but they are words which people with our flawed record must learn to say from the heart. Otherwise, there is no hope. Human relationships will be savaged and our relationship with God will simply be terminated.

It is impossible to estimate just how many of the Lord's disciples today are destroying themselves because they lack either the humility or the courage to repent of sins against others and seek their forgiveness. The dark secret of their guilt rests like some massive stone in their hearts, stultifying worship and sucking the spiritual life out of them (Psa 32.3–4). If such is the case with you, quit parading the corpse in worship assemblies. Put an end to self-defense and self-justification. Go quickly and be reconciled to the one you have injured. The pain of repentance will be small indeed compared to the agony of continued guilt and alienation.

"Agree with your adversary quickly" (Matt 5.25). Playing still on the Pharisees' narrow concern with civil penalties, Jesus continues to make His point in the metaphor of the civil court. To understand this as mere prudential advice to settle "out of court" in order to escape the vagaries of corrupt judges would not only trivialize the Lord's words but it would also set them at odds with their context. Jesus is still treating the issue of sins against others. The "adversary" is not the one who has brought some baseless charge against you but one whom you have injured, defrauded or defamed and whose case is just. Pride may counsel you to brazen it out, but Jesus urges a speedy reconciliation in view of a divine judgment which will be executed without mercy (Matt 5.26). It is just this kind of judgment that sinful men cannot bear. Better that we seek mercy hastily while the opportunity is open to us. Even divine clemency has its limits.

The War Against Lust

"Whoever looks at a woman to lust for her has already committed adultery" (Matt 5.28). These are radical words and even kingdom citizens must struggle not to resist. Their severe probing of the heart brings pain as the Son of God touches the raw nerves of our moral diseases. Jesus, having dealt with the problem of hate and malice, now addresses the problem of lust. The Pharisees had certainly treated the issue of adultery, but only superficially. Their concern was to avoid a capital offense (Lev 20.10; Deut 22.22). One can almost hear the way they said, "You shall not *commit* adultery" (Exod 20.14). Jesus, in contrast, tracks the sin of adultery to its lair (Matt 15.19). As the hatred of the heart is murder, so is the unbridled lust of the heart adultery.

This principle was not an obscure part of the Mosaic covenant. The tenth commandment pointedly said, "You shall not covet your neighbor's wife" (Exod 20.17). Paul, while still a stranger to the gospel, and a Pharisee, had been severely penetrated by this command (Rom 7.7). Even Job, a man who apparently lived before the law, understood this ethical truth. "I have made a covenant with my eyes," he said, "Why then should I look upon a young woman?" (Job 31.1).

Though some extended application might be made from this passage to the raw and unprincipled carnal desire which some single person might harbor for someone similarly unattached, Jesus' use of the word "adultery" makes clear that His present concern is with that illicit desire which violates the very spirit of the marriage covenant (2 Cor 11.2–3). The Lord's concern in this whole section is with our duty to love others. No married person can do justice to his mate while given over to unrestrained desire for another. Though yet a matter of the mind it is called what it is—sin.

The Lord is not dealing here with the mere momentary passing of desire through the mind; otherwise there would be no distinction between temptation and sin. (We should not be aghast at the suggestion that the lust of the flesh might have made its approach to the mind of our Savior while He remained sinless, Heb 4.15.) The words, "looks at a woman to lust for her," help us to understand the exact nature of the transgression. This is not a fleeting thought but the gathering up of one's mind for the purpose of lusting. The Greek text describes a person who directs his thoughts or turns his mind to a thing; in this case, lusting after a woman (or a man). Obviously, we do not look at everything we see. The eye takes in a vast panorama and it is left for the mind to focus the attention. David's sin was not in *seeing* the unclothed Bathsheba but in *looking upon* her, setting his mind and ultimately his unbridled lust upon her (2 Sam 11.2–5). David wanted the opportunity to possess Bathsheba, and found it. His violation of Exodus 20.17 would have been no less had that opportunity never presented itself.

Although the English word "lust" accurately connotes the sensual overtones of the Greek verb *(epithumeo),* it may lack the attendant thought of possession which is inherent in it (Guelich, *The Sermon on the Mount,* p 194). The sin being described by Jesus is the calculated cultivation of the desire to possess one to whom you have no right. If this sin is to be escaped, the very first approach of such thoughts must be decisively rejected, before they can take possession of the mind and will. In the language of an old proverb: "You cannot keep the birds from flying over your head but you can keep them from building a nest in your hair." If we find difficulty in distinguishing between the temptation and the sin in this case it is far wiser to err on the side of caution than on the side of recklessness.

The war of the kingdom citizen with lust in these times is destined to be severe and hard-fought. We are not going to easily escape the miasma of lasciviousness, fornication and adultery that has descended on this generation. Let no disciple be smug (1 Cor 10.12). There are no societal restraints to lean on. Our strength and defense must reside wholly in our own deep and unshakable resolve to keep ourselves pure for the Lord's sake. In the final analysis that is where the issue of our faithfulness in the kingdom has always been decided. "Keep your heart with all diligence, for out of it spring the issues of life" (Prov 4.23).

Radical Surgery

"**If your right eye causes you to sin, pluck it out**" (Matt 5.29). Matthew 5.29–30 contains two of the most startling sentences in the Gospels. In words brutally plain Jesus speaks of the harsh alternatives open to a man confronted with total annihilation because of the danger presented by a treasured part of his body. Here the threat lies in the right eye and the right hand. Later, in a different context, Jesus repeats His illustration, adding the "foot" (Matt 18.8–9; Mark 9.43–47). The language may be shocking but the situation is not far-fetched. In the days of more primitive medicine many a gangrenous limb was cut away by surgeons in order to save the life of the sufferer, and modern medicine will still counsel the same traumatic surgery when a part of the body threatens the life of the whole. Men have even been known to perform this surgery on themselves when an arm or leg, ensnared by machinery, is dragging them to their death. It is a radical step, but eminently sensible.

This passage is the place where those who staunchly affirm their confidence in the *literal* interpretation of all Scripture will have to take a very deep breath. There can be no question that Jesus builds His message on a truth from the world of the flesh, but it is evident from the context that His language has application to the world of the spirit (if the right eye was removed the sinner could still lust just as effectively with his left). In these grim words the true depth of change which the Son of God is demanding finds dramatic expression. In the same vein Jesus spoke of our coming to Him as a crucifixion (Matt 16.24–25; see Gal 2.20) and Paul provides a commentary on Matt 5.29–30 in his words to the Colossians: "Therefore put to death your members which are on the earth: fornication, uncleanness, passion, evil desire..." (Col 3.5).

Though our Lord is not speaking here of physical mutilation, which would be wholly ineffectual against the motions of the heart, we should not presume that the figurative intent of His words makes them any less intensely painful. There are "parts" of us—affections, habits, attitudes, values, relationships—which have become by long cultivation so intimately a part of our personality that their removal will make the actual excision of an eye or hand seem conservative. Most of us have spent a long time learning how to be selfish and lustful. We should not expect the end of these things to come without trauma. Shrieks of anguish may arise from somewhere within us as in penitence we apply the gospel knife. But some pain is good pain. "For he who has suffered in the flesh has ceased from sin" (1 Pet 4.1). We can choose to avoid this suffering but our cherished lusts will destroy us like some awful gangrene of the soul.

The radical and decisive nature of this renunciation is stressed by Jesus' instruction not only to gouge out or cut off the offending member but to *cast it away*. The separation is to be absolute and final, not gradual. This is a radical solution but it ought to be received with joy instead of horror. What man whose disease has given him the sentence of death without recourse would not rejoice to hear that the sacrifice of one part of his body, however dear, could save his life? Even the detailing of the wrenching pain which would ensue could not rob this delivered man of his sense of relief. The only reason that we do not receive with happiness a message of similar import for our souls is that we have not yet comprehended the full extent of our ultimate jeopardy without it. "What shall a man give in exchange for his life?"

Though Jesus could have spoken these arresting words with good purpose at any time during this section of His discourse, He chose to utter them in connection with the temptation to lust and adultery. Why? Would we be wrong to conclude that He did so because kingdom citizens will know no more radical challenge to the purity of their hearts than in the matter of sensual desire? "How the mighty have fallen!" David, who yielded no ground on other battlefields, was felled easily by the subtle lure of another man's wife. Many a mighty man of valor has been reduced to jelly by the same trial. We will be consummate fools if we do not treat this temptation with utmost gravity and walk in its presence with prayerful circumspection. In the face of the Lord's stern warning we continue to marvel at the careless familiarity with which some married disciples treat those of the opposite sex, and the circumstantial pitfalls to which they heedlessly expose themselves. Even while many of the churches are reeling from one celebrated case of adultery to another we seem at times to have learned nothing. The context of this same metaphor as used by the Lord in the latter part of Matthew (Matt 18.8–9) and in Mark (Mark 9.43–47) suggests that one possible meaning of the offending "eye" and "hand" is *an occasion of stumbling*. If such is the case, we are being charged not only to remove the sinful act (whether physical adultery or adultery of the heart) but any circumstances or relationships which could easily lead to it. Paul puts it plainly: "Flee sexual immorality" (1 Cor 6.18). How desperately Christians of this generation need to listen.

The Treachery of Divorce

"Whoever divorces his wife." The subject of divorce can fill the heart of a preacher with dread. More than two thirds of the preachers for America's largest Protestant denomination recently admitted that they had never spoken on the subject. The issue of divorce (and remarriage) touches the lives of men and women intimately and often painfully. Yet those who come to the kingdom must not expect that any part of their lives will escape the influence of the King; nor should they desire it since His commands are not arbitrary (1 John 5.3) but are always for our good (Deut 6.24). However agonizing this teaching may be to us, there is no place for the true disciple to hide from its implications.

In Matthew 5.31–32 Jesus continues His discussion of marriage and the principle of love which He began in verse 27.

"Furthermore it has been said, 'Whoever divorces his wife, let him give her a certificate of divorce'" (Matt 5.31). This Pharisaic tradition which the Lord cites is based on a distortion of Deuteronomy 24.1–4, the first part of which says, "When a man takes a wife and marries her, and it happens that she finds no favor in his eyes because he has found some uncleanness in her, and he writes her a certificate of divorce, puts it in her hand, and sends her out of his house." The meaning of these verses had been hotly disputed among the rabbinical schools. Shammai, insisting on a criminal and legal cause for the divorce, emphasized the words "some uncleanness," and limited it to adultery. Hillel stressed the words "finds no favor in his eyes," and allowed divorce for anything displeasing to the husband. Rabbi Akiba went even further, permitting divorce if a man simply found a more appealing woman.

From other information available to us in the New Testament it is evident that the Pharisees shared the very loose views of Hillel if not worse ones (Matt 19.3, 7), and were far less concerned about the reason for the divorce and its unholy consequences on the victim than for the following of proper forms. Their obsession with legal niceties to the complete disregard of moral principle is again revealed. The Pharisees viewed divorce as a right, and saw the words of Moses as a command (Matt 19.7) rather than a permissive allowance. By so doing they had wholly misapprehended the law and its purpose.

God's attitude toward divorce had been made abundantly clear in the Old Testament whose canon had virtually closed with the ringing words, "For the LORD God of Israel says that He hates divorce" (Mal 2.16). Consistent with that divine sentiment the words of Deuteronomy 24.1–4 were intended to put a check on already rampant divorce, not to introduce and encourage it. Jesus describes the teaching of the law on divorce as a concession to Israel's "hardness of heart" (Matt 19.8), not surely a "hardness" of stubborn rebellion, which would have been intolerable (Heb 3.7–11), but one borne of spiritual backwardness (Mark 6.52). The law worked its restraint on divorce in three ways. It limited divorce to certain causes (Jesus' contrast of His own teaching of divorce for fornication alone with that of the law would indicate that Moses allowed more than one reason for divorce, Matt 19.7–9). It required that a certificate of divorce be given to the wife (usually in the presence of two witnesses [Matt 1.19] and containing the words, "Lo thou art free to marry any man"). And it gave a compelling argument against hasty and intemperate action by forbidding the husband to ever again take his divorced companion (once she had remarried) to wife.

"But I say to you that whoever divorces his wife for any reason except sexual immorality causes her to commit adultery" (Matt 5.32). In His response to the Pharisaic gloss about divorce Jesus is primarily concerned with principle rather than procedure. Any man who casts out his faithful wife had acted without love and must share in the guilt of her adultery (her remarriage is assumed). The only exception is divorce for fornication which would preclude her husband making her what she had already become. In this context it seems evident that although "fornication" *(porneia)* can cover illicit sexual union both in and out of marriage the Lord uses it here of sin within the marriage covenant rather than before it.

The current disposition of some to justify divorce for any reason if there is no remarriage causes me to stress that the sin Jesus speaks of here rests in divorce, not remarriage. Such a divorce is wrong on three counts. It is wrong because it shows no love for the mate. It is wrong because it could push the divorced mate into a damning relationship. And it is wrong because it could involve another otherwise innocent person in adultery. To this we feel compelled to add that even in cases where fornication has occurred the redemptive love of the kingdom would seem to counsel mercy and reconciliation where possible. Divorce was never a commandment. Love is.

Finally, it is evident that Jesus in His answer to the Pharisees has traveled beyond Deuteronomy, even properly understood, and has stated the law of the kingdom of heaven which rests upon God's will "from the beginning" (Matt 19.8–9). The law of Moses would have allowed the divorced woman to remarry; the law of the kingdom will not.

Not Oaths, but Truth

In Matthew 5.33–37 Jesus presents the fourth of His six antitheses which contrast Pharisaic perversions of the law with the righteousness of the kingdom of heaven. The exact words of the traditional teaching which Jesus cites (Matt 5.33) are not found anywhere in the Old Testament but were fashioned from statements like that of Leviticus 19.12: "And you shall not swear by My name falsely, nor shall you profane the name of your God" (see Exod 20.17; Deut 6.11; Num 30.2).

The law's approach to oaths was similar to its approach to divorce. The Mosaic covenant did not ordain divorce but sought to regulate and restrain what was already prevalent. Correspondingly, the law did not originate oaths or command Israel to swear but directed that any oaths taken should be by the name of God (Deut 6.13; 10.20) and must not be false (Lev 19.12; Zech 8.17; Mal 3.5). But these restrictions were never intended to be understood as permission to lie when not under oath. God's hatred of all lies is made abundantly clear in the Old Testament (Prov 6.17; 12.22).

Unfortunately, the Pharisees, instead of finding in God's regulations concerning swearing an appeal for constant truthfulness, saw rather a loophole for deceit. The thrust of their tradition was: "Don't perjure yourself when the name of God is involved." "Unto the Lord" was the operative phrase of their perversion. To facilitate their dishonesty the Pharisees made sophistic distinctions between binding and non-binding oaths (Matt 23.16–22). These hypocrites had a fine concern to avoid perjury (as they defined it) but no commitment to honesty, truthfulness and neighbor love.

It is one of the tragedies of this section of the sermon that it has been reduced to little more than a battleground over the permissibility of judicial oaths. The evil which Jesus attacks in His prohibition of swearing (Matt 5.34) is not oaths, but deception. He sweeps away the vain oaths of the Pharisees with their deceitful subtleties by observing that there is nothing by which they might swear (heaven, earth, Jerusalem, their own head) which was not at last tied directly to God and His power (Matt 5.34–36; 23.16–22). The Lord is simply stressing the essential truth that every word we utter is "before God" and subject to divine judgment (Matt 12.36–37). A simple emphatic "yes" or "no" puts men under no less obligation to tell the truth and honor their promises than the most stringent oath. Oaths were never intended to heighten the swearer's obligation to tell the truth (that existed already) but to give greater assurance to those who received them (Heb 6.13–18).

What are the practical lessons to learn from all this? Some have seen here a stern warning against profanity. A good lesson on that subject would certainly be in order. We are without question a blasphemous generation. Jaded with small blasphemies and seeking bigger ones, we treat with urbane amusement the sacrilegious savaging of words like God, Christ, heaven, hell, salvation and damnation. Our mindless uttering of holy names has cost us our sense of reverence and with it our sense of humanity. But profanity is not our Lord's primary concern here. His concern is honesty—total, absolute honesty.

What we owe our brother and our neighbor is truth in all our words or no words at all. There are many temptations to lie and be faithless. Hatred, guilt and covetousness move us to stretch the truth until it snaps. Selfishness or lust entreats us to break the solemn vows of marriage. Thoughtlessness prompts us to forget as unimportant the day-to-day promises we make to others. Some Christians have lied away their integrity by unfounded accusations and unsupported claims. Others have promised away their honor with unkept commitments. Such behavior is unacceptable in a kingdom citizen. We serve a God who cannot lie (Tit 2.1) and must bring to His service a transparent honesty and truthfulness (Col 3.9; Eph 4.15, 25).

But we must not close this study without dealing with an obvious and unresolved question. Does not Jesus by the words, "Do not swear at all," prohibit the taking of any kind of oath? There has long been in my heart a ready reception for such a conclusion, but the broad context of the New Testament raises some serious questions about it. We are not so much troubled by the realization that God (Acts 2.30; Heb 6.17; 7.20–21), His Son (Matt 26.63–64) and His angels (Rev 10.5–6) have sworn oaths, as we are by the fact that the epistles of Paul are fairly sprinkled with oath-like expressions we can explain no other way (Rom 1.9; 9.1; 2 Cor 1.23; 11.31; Gal 1.20; Phil 1.8; *et al.*).

How can we reconcile Paul's clear practice with Jesus' prohibition? First, we believe, by recognizing that some apparently absolute statements turn out not to be when the whole of Scripture is to be considered (Mark 10.11–12 and Matt 19.9; Matt 5.42 and 2 Thes 3.10). And then by realizing that Jesus is treating in this context the lying oaths of the Pharisees and not the solemn oaths of those who would tell the truth under any circumstances but find that at times others are in need of special assurance. Each Christian must weigh this matter carefully, remembering that he is not compelled to swear, but that he is always compelled to speak the truth.

An Idea Whose Time Has Not Come

If Jesus was attempting to formulate ethical principles which would catch the spirit of His age, He certainly was a failure. His teachings were alien and untimely and stirred animosity even in the nation of Israel. But the Son of God had always known that "the time" for His teaching would never come in history. As He once said to His then unbelieving brothers: "My time has not yet come, but your time is always ready. The world cannot hate you, but it hates Me because I testify of it that its works are evil" (John 7.6–7).

The ethical teachings of Jesus are no less alien to our own age, and there is no more radical expression of kingdom righteousness than in the last two of His six great contrasts between the distortions of the Pharisees and the will of God (Matt 5.38–48). These words have stirred more controversy than all the rest of the sermon put together and many efforts to explain them have only served to explain them away and strip them of all force. Perhaps it would be helpful as an introduction to Jesus' teaching on the love of one's enemies to look at some of the controversy that has surrounded them.

There has been wide disagreement over how broad an application ought to be made to the principle of neighbor love. Some have said that it applies only to "personal" relationships and others have contended that it must apply to every facet of the Christian's life. In support of the more dominant view that narrows application to "one-on-one" neighbor relations Carl F. H. Henry has written the following: "In Christian businessmen's circles it is often said that the Sermon on the Mount is the superlative code of ethics for success in business. But the fact is that a big business man who conducts his trade by the ethics of the Sermon—giving two garments when one is asked free, not resisting violence—would soon find himself hopelessly in debt or completely out of business. ...A nation which runs its affairs by the law of neighbor relations—acting only on the principle of unrequited love, giving twice as much as its enemies demand, and committed to non-resistance of aggressions against it—is in process of national suicide" (*Christian Personal Ethics*, pp 322–323).

Dietrich Bonhoeffer gives expression to the opposing view in his little book *The Cost of Discipleship:* "This saying of Jesus removes the Church from the sphere of politics and law. The Church is not to be a national community like the old Israel, but a community of believers without political or national ties. The Old Israel has been both—the chosen people of God and a national community, and it was therefore His will that they should meet force with force. But with the church it is different: it has abandoned political and national status, and therefore it must patiently endure aggression. ...But this distinction between person and office is wholly alien to the teaching of Jesus. He addresses His disciples as men who have left all to follow Him, and the precept of nonviolence applies equally to private life and official duty. He is the Lord of life, and demands undivided allegiance. Furthermore, when it comes to practice, this distinction raises insoluble difficulties. Am I ever acting only as a private person or only in an official capacity? ...Am I not always an individual, face to face with Jesus, even in the performance of my official duties?" (pp 121–124).

Does the principle of love apply to every aspect of the Christian's dealings with others or is it limited to certain personal dealings only? This is a question that has been raised again and again over the centuries and it is the one that the citizen of the kingdom must wrestle with and decide. There is no place of refuge from this very practical issue.

Questions have also been raised over whether the Christian is forbidden all right of self-defense in personal relationships or if he is required to submit to evil only when attacked or mistreated for the gospel's sake. Martin Luther had some interesting comments on this issue in his *Table Talks:* "If anyone breaks into my home, tries to do violence to my family or to myself or to cause harm, I am bound to defend myself and them in my capacity as master of the house and a head of the family. If brigands or murderers have tried to harm me or do me wrongful violence I should have defended myself and resisted them in the name of the prince whose subject I am. …I must help the prince to purge his country of bad subjects. And if I have the strength to cut this bandit's throat, it is my duty to take the knife to him. …But if I am attacked on account of the divine word, in my capacity as a preacher, then I must endure it and leave God to punish him and avenge me."

All this should help us see that we have some difficult questions to wrestle with in our effort to understand the true demand of kingdom righteousness. And while we struggle earnestly to understand and apply these challenging teachings we must constantly guard ourselves against the temptation to simply rationalize away anything that seems burdensome and unappealing. We cannot discount our Lord's teachings merely because they seem revolutionary. Clearly there has never been a teacher in human history more at odds with everything men in their wisdom have thought to be right than Jesus of Nazareth.

Vengeance Is Not Our Business

"But I tell you not to resist an evil person" (Matt 5.39). Though much controversy surrounds this section of the sermon, our first task is to lay issues aside and attempt to understand in its most elemental form the point that Jesus is making.

In Matthew 5.38–42 Jesus broadens the scope and deepens the application of the principle of neighbor love. He has now moved from dealing with the problem of evil in ourselves to the challenge of wrestling with evil in others. It is one thing for the kingdom citizen to withhold all injury from the innocent, but what does love demand of him when others, far from innocent, attempt to abuse and injure him?

The Pharisees had worked out the problem nicely. They simply picked up on an Old Testament statute governing the amount of retribution that might be exacted in law for a particular injury done and turned it into a *right* to vengeance upon their adversaries.

The purpose of the Old Testament law of retribution was likely twofold. It was intended to restrain and deter the practice of evil (Deut 19.20–21). It also served to control the disposition of men to exact in anger a punishment disproportionate to the injury suffered (Exod 21.23–24). Anger at injustice suffered can so easily burn out of control and exact wholly exorbitant punishment. God's law to Israel intended that such excesses which only initiate an endless cycle of hatred and violence should be restrained. It is also very important to note that this justice was not to be administered privately but meted out only by the appointed judges of Israel (Deut 19.18).

The Pharisees evidently saw in the words of the law they so often quoted ("An eye for an eye, and a tooth for a tooth") a right of personal vengeance. Instead of understanding this as a statement of the maximum possible retribution under law, a control on excess, they held it as their personal minimum right. Like Shakespeare's Shylock these merciless hypocrites demanded their "pound of flesh."

In contrast to the teaching of the Pharisees which established the right of personal revenge and retaliation in kind Jesus says "not to resist an evil person." He then follows His statement of principle with four very dramatic illustrations of it.

It is imperative at the outset that we consider Jesus' prohibition (against resisting evil) in the context of His sermon and, to an extent, in the broader context of the New Testament. Jesus' concern in this whole section (Matt 5.21–48) is the working out of the principle of love for others. In Luke's account of the sermon Jesus' illustrations of His principle are preceded by the command to love one's enemies and followed by the admonition, "And just as you want men to do to you, you also do to them likewise" (Luke 6.27–31). Perhaps this will help us to understand that the Lord is not issuing a doctrine of mere non-resistance but simply using a series of very arresting statements to accentuate our obligation never to retaliate for wrongs done us, and never to withhold good from those who have injured us unjustly. We must not make these statements walk on all-fours.

When Jesus instructs His disciples not to resist evil, He is *not* telling them never to do anything to restrain evil in others. Such a wooden interpretation would prevent even a word of reproof. The Lord taught otherwise in Matthew 18.15–17 and Himself rebuked the officer who wrongfully struck Him during His trial (John 18.23). What our Savior is concerned with in these verses is that we should never resist evil *with evil*. This is exactly how Paul states the principle in Romans: "Repay no one evil for evil. …Do not be overcome by evil, but overcome evil with good" (Rom 12.17, 21). This is the natural working out of the command to love one's neighbor as oneself and the appeal to do toward others what we would have done to ourselves. Whatever we do in response to their evil must be done *in love* for *them*, not out of some desire for revenge or concern for *self*-defense. It seems to me that this principle would not preclude even the use of some rather strong means to restrain another from inflicting wrongful injury but it must always be administered out of love for the offender and never selfishly or vengefully.

So in these pointedly dramatic statements of Jesus in which He has certainly gotten our attention He is telling us: that it is better to turn the other cheek to the person who has struck you than to do evil to him; that it is better to give your cloak to the man who has wrongfully sued you for your coat than to wrong him or withhold what he really needs; that it is better to go two miles with the man who has wrongfully compelled you to assist him than to do evil to him or fail to give the assistance that he truly needs; that it is better to give aid to the man who has treated you badly than to withhold what he genuinely requires in his time of trouble.

If this sounds to you as if we are draining the force from these commands, please remember that Jesus' instruction to "give to him who asks you" is not without reservation. Paul said, "If anyone will not work, neither shall he eat" (2 Thes 3.10). Yet even Paul's charge is not punitive but motivated by love. And remember, too, that we will have more than enough to challenge us in keeping our hearts free from all selfishness as we determine how we are to treat *with love* those who deal unjustly and often brutally with us.

The Unthinkable Commandment

With every advancing sentence since verse 21 Jesus has taken an ever larger bite out of the human ego. Every new contrast between the popular Pharisaic perversions and the real demand of kingdom righteousness has served to heighten the moral challenge. What the Lord at last commands in the sixth and last of these antitheses must have stunned His audience (Matt 5.43–48). He had spoken the inconceivable when He said, **"but I say to you, love your enemies"** (Matt 5.44). To many of His listeners such counsel must have seemed not only unthinkable, but impossible—and contrary to the very concept of justice.

Now for the first time in the sermon Jesus has spoken the word which best sums up the principle underlying the whole of His message. He has led His hearers up an ascending plane from what love prohibits in the treatment of others (even those who abuse us) to what love demands of us positively. And who among His audience then or now could have anticipated that the journey would not be finished until He had demanded of them the hardest thing of all—to love the very ones we are most drawn to hate—our enemies. Finally the Lord has left no room for "self" at all.

"Enemy" was hardly a foreign idea to first-century Jews. By Jesus' time there was a palpable enmity that had attached itself to the partitioning wall that was the law (Eph 2.14–15). The people of Israel had suffered much from a hostile world and often looked with disdain upon the ignorant paganism and egregious immorality of the Gentiles. The Gentiles were not slow to return the favor. The Pharisees, with their separatist fervor, were not ignorant of the law's demand that the sons of the covenant were to love their neighbor as themselves (Lev 19.18), but they understood that obligation to end at the borders of Israel. There were plenty to hate beyond the pale and many in the nation held that it was not only their privilege but their obligation to do so. The fact that the Pharisees were aware of the command to love but floundered on the definition of "neighbor" is evidenced by the conversation with a certain lawyer (Luke 10.25–29). The lawyer knew the formula but was yet to make a proper application.

But how and why did the teachers in Israel come to conclude that the law commanded hatred for the enemy? It might have been the "holy wars" of extermination which God commanded Israel to wage against the Canaanites (Deut 20.16–18), or the imprecatory psalms ("Do not I hate them, O LORD, who hate You? …I hate them with perfect hatred; I count them my enemies," Psa 139.21–22. Note especially Psa 109). Yet, however difficult and perplexing be the problems which these facts present, the law did not distinguish in the matter of neighbor love between the Israelite and the stranger (Lev 19.18 with 19.33–34) and it did not counsel hatred and vengeance for the enemy (Exod 23.4–5). Even Job, whose times most likely antedate the law, understood the sin of rejoicing over the calamity of an enemy (Job 31.29–30). It has always impressed me that when Paul sought to instruct his brethren in their treatment of enemies he felt no need for some new revelation but drew easily upon the book of Proverbs: "If your enemy is hungry, feed him; if he is thirsty, give him a drink" (Rom 12.20; Prov 25.21). There is no portion of the Old Testament which more directly addresses the problem of Israel's attitude toward her enemies than the book of Jonah. The Assyrians were a brutal people, enemies of God and men, but Jehovah loved them and He intended that His servant Jonah should do the same (Jon 4.9–11).

Still, if after all this, we find ourselves hard pressed to believe that the law did not counsel enmity toward enemies, we are left to trust the Son of God who rebukes this idea as a misconception of the law and wholly inconsistent with the nature and purpose of God. It was just such teaching as this that made the nation so unprepared for the coming of the peaceable kingdom.

Had Jesus told His followers to love their "neighbor" they might well have continued in the old narrow ways, missing completely this love's unique nature. But when He teaches them to love their *enemies* they may be startled but they will certainly be instructed. As Kierkegaard has observed, the gospel has made it forever impossible for anyone to be mistaken about the identity of his neighbor. If we are to love our enemies, then there will certainly be no member of the human race, however different, however distant, however vile, to which we will not owe the best we can give him.

A Different Kind of Love

The love of which Jesus calls His followers is one which surpasses the ordinary. Old "loves" that we have known are an insufficient preface for the new lessons we must learn. Family ties, devotion between friends, passion between lovers are "natural" affections so common to men that their absence is a sign of subhuman degradation (Rom 1.31). Loving those who love them gives no special distinction to the sons of the kingdom. As Jesus observes, even such "low types" as the publicans and the Gentiles were capable of such an exchange of kindnesses (Matt 5.46–47).

The "love" of kingdom righteousness is extraordinary, not merely in intensity, but in kind. It is love of a different and higher order. Much of the difficulty we suffer in our efforts to understand it comes from the mistaken presumption that it is of the same genre as our natural affections, built upon strong mutuality, deep attraction, shared experiences and interests. How, we ask, can we feel a warm affection for those who are doing their dead level best to destroy us? Our enemies are not only unattractive to us but their behavior is despicable. We are repelled by both their actions and their persons.

Clearly the old rules do not apply here. A love for one's adversaries cannot be built upon emotion. The love that can embrace its enemies does not originate on earth. Men, even in their most heroic moments, have only managed to love the lovable (Rom 5.7). God, on the other hand, has consistently loved His enemies, sending rain and sunlight upon both good and evil (Matt 5.45). This divine good will has nothing to do with some attractive quality found in us. We have succeeded to a man in making ourselves morally repugnant (Ecc 7.20; Rom 3.9–18), and it is highly unlikely that we shall ever in this life understand how fully His holy nature is repelled by our ungodly ways. The yearning of God for men arises, as it must, from His own gracious character and will. In His mercy He wills to do good to those whose very lives are an offense to His nature. He has loved the unlovable. How truly Paul has written, "But God demonstrates His own love toward us, in that while we were still sinners, Christ died for us" (Rom 5.8).

The power that opens to citizens of the kingdom of heaven the ability to love in such a selfless way is the example of their Father. There is an awesome strength about the One who has created all things. The heavens declare His glory (Psa 19.1). The universe testifies to His everlasting power and deity (Rom 1.20). But it is not in the greatness of His creative power that we truly know God (1 Kgs 19.11–12). The final, full revelation of God was reserved for One who came in "weakness" (1 Cor 1.27) and emptied Himself for the sake of others (Phil 2.5f). Jesus alone has revealed the Father in completeness (John 1.18) and only when we have seen Him have we seen His Father (John 14.6–7). We have never looked more squarely into the face of the living God than when we stand by faith at the foot of the cross and hear His Son plead for mercy upon the ungodly men who are murdering Him. Here is power. Here is deity. We do not deny His absolute physical might. We cannot resist His wisdom. His perfect righteousness fills us with reverential awe. But when we have found access by Christ into the "deep things of God" (1 Cor 2.10) we will know that there is no truer description of the divine character than John's brief affirmation, "God is love" (1 John 4.8).

Men who have been the beneficiaries of such an undeserved graciousness ought to be able to understand and apply it to others. Indeed, "We love Him because He first loved us" (1 John 4.19). But this love is a love of the will, not of the emotions. Our Savior is not asking that we have a warm affection for our enemies. In reality, our success in truly loving them will be directly dependent on our ability to detach ourselves from their behavior and respond to their true need rather than their conduct. In his commentary on the Gospel of Matthew, William Barclay has given a most apt description of this heavenly kind of love: "Agape [love] does not mean a feeling of the heart, which we cannot help, and which comes unbidden and unsought; it means a determination of the mind, whereby we achieve this unconquerable good will even toward those who hurt and injure us." This is the kind of moral determination which must come at last to be the foundation of all our other loves. It must be the sustaining force upon which is built the deep affections of marriage and the family, the selfless comradeship of friends, and above all, the fellowship of the saints.

"Therefore you shall be perfect, just as your Father in heaven is perfect" (Matt 5.48). There is something immeasurably grand as well as deeply disturbing about being called upon to be like God. The possibility thrills while the challenge frightens. The perfection which Jesus both promises and commands for His disciples does not refer to God's sinless righteousness but to the fullness and completeness of His love. Our imperfect, selective good will must be enlarged to encompass all men. Such a love will not be bought at a cheap price. Pain and agony are in the process. But we must grow up to be like our Father or yield the right to be called His children (1 John 4.7–8).

Must We Always Love Our Enemies?

The love demanded of the Lord's disciple is radical. It is far more than the civility that keeps one from exacting personal vengeance upon his enemies. It is the positive good will which causes him to pray and work for the ultimate good of his adversaries (Matt 5.44; Luke 6.35). It is not surprising, therefore, that men have often struggled against its impact.

Must the kingdom citizen always act for the eternal well-being of others? Must this be his attitude when his property or even his life is being threatened? Must the disciple as peace officer, soldier, father, mother, *etc.*, continually govern his behavior by this selfless and redemptive principle?

This question has rent the centuries with controversy, some arguing that the love principle of the sermon is absolute and universal, others defending various exceptions. For two centuries after the death of the apostles no extant writer approved of the Christian's participation in war. Following the reign of Constantine when the now "Christian" empire was under attack by barbarian hordes, Augustine and others, while still counseling personal nonviolence, permitted, and often urged, the Christian to participate in "just wars" as agents of the civil state. Augustine defended such a war as a defensive war of last resort waged by constituted authority for just causes, by just means, and for just ends (Roland Bainton, *Christian Attitudes Toward War and Peace*, pp 66, 67, 89–100). The leading voices of the Reformation held the "just war" view, justifying the Christian's involvement in military combat by the wars of Israel and making a distinction between the disciple as an individual and the disciple as an agent of the state.

There is no easy way to resolve the question of whether the Christian is always to love his enemies, involving us as it does in the difficult issues of the Christian's relation to the state and the right of individual self-defense. Nonetheless, we believe that the answer to the question we have raised should be an unqualified "yes."

When one argues the unrestricted right of personal self-defense against the teachings of Matthew 5.38–48, the Lord's command to work the ultimate good of one's enemies has been effectively nullified. Excluding the right of self-defense in cases of attack for the gospel's sake leaves the Christian in the virtually impossible position of having to quickly and accurately ascertain the motive of his assailant. We are content to say that any self-defense consistent with the eternal good of our adversary is wholly permissible (Matt 7.12).

When one argues that the wars of Israel should establish that a people commanded to love their enemies can also wage war against them, it should at least be noted that these were wars of unprovoked aggression, and often extermination, which were fought at God's command (Exod 23.31–32; Deut 20.10–19). They speak more to God's right of judgment upon the wicked than to any case for "just war." It is difficult, if not impossible, to compare modern wars with the wars of Israel (Clouse, *War: Four Christian Views*, p 10).

The waging of a "just war" by unconverted men has always been more dream than reality. There is hardly a modern war, perhaps none, in which both sides have not in some clear way violated the "just war" model. Modern warfare has forced us to ask how justice can be meted out to the guilty and the innocent preserved by the blanket bombing of whole cities or the incineration of whole populations in an atomic holocaust. And, even if this were not true, there would remain the impossible burden which this view places on the Christian to know things about international conflicts which often do not become generally known until years afterward. No nation openly wages an unjust war. Justice is always the cry by which they stir their citizenry to arms.

At the extreme, we may be dealing in the civil state with an instrument of God which exists by His *permissive* authority (Rom 13.1; John 19.11) and which He uses as a "vessel of wrath" to maintain order in an ungodly world (Isa 10.5–7, 12; Jer 25.9;

Isa 14.4–6; Dan 4.17, 24–25; Isa 44.28; 45.1). At the least, we are dealing with an institution under a limited commission to act with justice in punishing the evildoer and protecting the innocent (Rom 13.1–7; 1 Pet 2.13–14). In neither case are we free to have a heedless relationship with civil authority, naively presuming that because God "ordained" it, it will always act in accordance with His will. The rulers of this world are most often portrayed in Scripture as the enemies of God's purposes (Psa 2.1–2; Dan 2.44). The rise of nationalism has often made mindless patriots of Christians in all countries, loyalty to the great King all but forgotten in the fever of a narrow partisanship. In no case are we allowed to turn our responsibility for moral choices over to the state and so escape the commitment we have made to love all men. The kingdom of heaven is a community from "every tribe and tongue and people and nation" which must fulfill the prophetic vision of a realm where men learn war no more (Isa 2.4; 11.9). If, in the service of kingdom righteousness, we forfeit our lives, nothing unexpected will have happened (Luke 14.26). In whatever circumstance we are found, we must love our enemies. If our circumstance prevents that, then our circumstance must be changed.

The Godward Life

The fifth chapter of Matthew contains a searching study of the righteousness of the kingdom of heaven (Matt 5.20–48). Jesus has begun by attacking the hypocritical posturing of the Pharisees at its most apparent point—their treatment of others. He makes clear that true righteousness is a piety that reaches to heart depth, probing at motives and attitudes and not merely words and deeds. Beneath all that He enjoins, though never explicitly stated, is the practical working out of the ancient command to love one's neighbor as oneself. Yet, if the Pharisees' loveless treatment of others was the most obvious manifestation of their spiritual bankruptcy, it was not here that their problems had begun. It is to that area where true righteousness begins that the Teacher now addresses Himself (Matt 6).

When Jesus concluded His teaching on neighbor love He had lifted His hearers to the very throne of God. **"Therefore you shall be perfect, just as your Father in heaven is perfect"** (Matt 5.48). It is here that the key to all piety, both moral and spiritual, rests—not in our relationship to others but in our relationship to God. "You shall love your neighbor as yourself" is the second of the great commandments; the first is "You shall love the LORD your God with all your heart" (Matt 22.35–37).

Men have struggled through the centuries to erect an ethical code apart from deity. But, as Schopenhauer once wrote: "to teach morality is easy. To find a basis for morality is hard." Such efforts have failed because in the absence of a moral God who cares about the behavior of His creatures all moral codes are arbitrary and meaningless. Indeed, if there is no such God it is inconceivable that man could even exist as a moral being. He should simply be incapable of entertaining ethical questions. The fact that man is moral speaks eloquently of the existence of a moral God.

But an ethic of human behavior, even so great and true a one as "You shall love your neighbor as yourself" cannot rest upon itself. It becomes meaningless and impossible apart from a deep commitment to the God upon whose nature and will the whole moral structure of the universe depends. Men who want to deal with morals must deal with God. That is the reason that the ethics of the kingdom of heaven are not possible of fulfillment save by those who are fit for the kingdom. They cannot be kept by unconverted men.

As chapter five ends, Jesus has already dealt in great detail with true righteousness, but the wellspring of that righteousness has only so far been hinted at. It is a heart righteousness—whole and undivided. But even as the chapter reaches its climax in the call to love one's enemies, we are made to cry out in despair, "How?!" And even while we are asking, our attention is drawn to heaven. It is God alone who can open up the possibility of such love among men. As John says, "We love Him because He first loved us" (1 John 4.19). Men, apart from God, may recognize in some measure the need to love one another in this very pure way, but they never will find within themselves the spiritual strength to do so. Only in an absolute commitment to God is it made possible.

It needs to be further understood that the ethical demands of the kingdom are not an end in themselves. As Jesus makes clear before introducing this new dimension of righteousness, the purpose of all ethical commands is to transform us into the likeness of our Father. So, if we have properly understood what Jesus is saying, the question with which we will end each day is not, "Have I committed murder or adultery or this or that?" but rather, "Has God been first in my life today?" "Have I kept His commandments?" "Have I been true to Him?" "Do I know Him better? Am I more like Him?"

Men have always been slow to understand that the most fundamental sin of all does not rest in our mistreatment of others but in our stubborn and pride-filled refusal to worship and honor God above all else. It is to this cosmic criminality that Paul speaks in Romans when he says of the pagan world: "Because, although they knew God, they did not glorify Him as God, nor were thankful, but became futile in their thoughts, and their foolish hearts were darkened" (Rom 1.21). It is because of this central crime that men have visited upon themselves such horrors of immorality and inhumanity (Rom 1.26–32), and not the reverse. The first task of men when seeking the righteousness of the kingdom of God is to deal with God Himself, and the only approach that has ever been acceptable to Him has been one of absolute humility and devotion.

The Problem of Pride

There is perhaps no greater rival for the love we owe to God than the human ego. Pride rests at the heart of sin's genius—the perverse desire of men to "be as God," to sit at the very center of everything. It is the death of that arrogant self-seeking mind, always exalting itself against the knowledge of God, which the gospel demands. This pride has about it a dark but spiritual quality. It is a desire of the mind, not of the flesh. The pleasure it finds is not in the evil done but in the very idea of rebellion. In his *Confessions* Augustine recalls a time in his youth when he and some of his friends robbed a neighbor's pear tree and fed most of the fruit to the pigs. It was not the pears that attracted him, he said, for there were better pears at home, but the thrill of taking the forbidden (Book II, chap. 4).

It is to this central and critical problem of pride that Jesus now turns His attention as He begins a study of three things which will subvert the kingdom citizen's true devotion to God (Matt 6.1–34). He introduces this first section (Matt 6.1–18) with a command which sets down a principle: **"Take heed that you do not do your righteousness before men, to be seen by them."** (The NKJV translates *charitable deeds* instead of *righteousness* but there is much stronger textual evidence for the latter.) He then illustrates His warning in three areas of religious piety—giving alms, prayer, and fasting.

One wonders at the outset what possible attraction almsgiving, prayer and fasting could have for the proud man since these are so related to humility before God and a selfless concern for others. Yet Jesus' warning makes clear that even religious piety can be turned through the mediation of pride into a heady, self-serving wickedness. What was there that drew the arrogant Pharisees to the Temple coffers and to frequent occasions of prayer and fasting (Luke 18.10–12)? It was the hope of self-elevation. For every ounce of apparent humility invested in these hypocrites reaped a pound of vainglory. In all of this we need to be warned that it is eminently possible to do the most noble thing for the most corrupt reason. Mere worship and generosity do not give a man sure refuge from evil. Satan will follow him right into the place of prayer and turn his very worship into sin. A man must keep his heart pure and his love true. God must be the object of everything.

This newly stated principle may at first seem at odds with Jesus' earlier charge to "let your light so shine *before men*" (Matt 5.16), but no real contradiction exists. There is a world of difference between doing good so as to reflect honor upon the God who made such goodness possible, and doing good so as to bring honor upon oneself. It is not being seen of men that concerns the Savior but the *desire to be seen* by them.

It may be unnecessary to state it, but the real issue here is not whether to please God or please men (a real problem, too) but whether to please God or please ourselves. It is this insidious delight with our own importance which poisons all our attempted piety. It is not for their good that we wish to be seen by men but for ours. The matter is easily resolved if we are humble enough to wish it. As Bonhoeffer expressed it, our light is to be seen of men but hidden from ourselves.

Pride, vainglory, is the very essence of the anti-God mentality. Men consumed by pride cannot love God. He is their enemy, their rival, the one who is standing where they want to stand. But it is not God alone that they cannot love. Pride at last prevents us from loving anyone. All men are seen as rivals for our position of honor. Others cannot be dealt with as friends, much less brothers. They can be tolerated only as servants to one's own vanity—tools to be discarded when they cease to serve their purpose well. Even the immoral worldling, caught up in the lust of the flesh, can enjoy some warm comradeship with his earthly fellows, but the proud man is denied even that.

The most crucial thing about pride is its subtlety. It can easily feed on the very efforts we make to stamp it out. First we are heedless in our open vanity. Then we repent of our arrogance. Then we proudly observe how bravely and completely we have left our old vain ways behind. Then we "see through" pride's trickery and again are filled with remorse. Then there comes slowly creeping in a feeling of smug self-satisfaction that we were so quick to catch pride in his subtle effort to recapture us. The process can go on endlessly. Pride doesn't mind giving ground as long as he holds the fort.

How then do we escape from this overweening self-esteem that makes it impossible for us to know God or love men? Not by concentrating on it. A man is not humble because he thinks so little of himself but because he does not think of himself at all. Pride dies only when self is forgotten; and we forget ourselves only in the face of a far greater loyalty and devotion. The old arrogant, vain self will have died when Christ so fills us that there is no longer any room for anything else (Gal 2.20; Col 3.3)—when we can say, almost without thinking, "Christ is all" (Col 3.11b). What a blessed thought!

The Sound of Trumpets

In the Sermon on the Mount Jesus does not establish any specific institutions of worship. Dealing simply with principles He illustrates them with expressions of religious piety already familiar to His audience (note Matt 5.23). Almsgiving, like prayer and fasting, was nothing new to His listeners. The law of Moses left no doubt about God's concern for the poor. Special provisions were made for their needs (Exod 23.11; Lev 19.9–10). A blessing was pronounced upon those who remembered them (Psa 41.1) and a curse upon those who did not (Prov 21.13). Yet, giving to the poor like all other expressions of devotion to God may be turned sour by a perverse motive. The absence of a Godward heart in what we do for others pollutes everything. Of course, if the love of money is a man's problem, giving all he owns to the poor could well be a solution (Matt 19.21), but the giving of alms is not necessarily an answer for the proud man (1 Cor 13.3). It may only serve to inflate his already enormous ego. It is to this issue that Jesus directs Himself in the first of His illustrations of religious hypocrisy (Matt 6.2–4).

"When you do a charitable deed, do not sound a trumpet before you" (Matt 6.2). Two powerful means of keeping the hounds of self-glory at bay are given here by the Savior. The first is, don't blow a horn every time you do something good. That is, don't advertise it to others. It is hardly likely that the hypocrites to which Jesus refers would be so blatant as to actually sound a trumpet every time they handed some poor soul a coin. The Lord is simply using a figure of speech. There are subtler and more effective ways of obtaining publicity for your generosity without looking like a fool.

When Jesus speaks of the "synagogues" and "streets" as being a popular site for hypocrite generosity, He is not saying that those locations were inappropriate for showing compassion. After all, it was in just such oft-frequented places that beggars sought help (John 9.1, 8; Acts 3.2). He is, rather, striking at the vainglorious disposition of some to perform exclusively in public.

But there is a subtler and more dangerous form of this ego disease—the willingness to give alms in quiet corners and then advertise it later in just the right offhanded sort of way. It is always so easy when talking "compassionately" of the needs of others to mention ever so casually what we have done for them. Jesus warns us in no uncertain terms to keep our mouths closed about the matter, content that our Father knows.

Kingdom citizens are people in search of godly character, not a mere reputation for piety. Yet, if heaven's righteousness is of the heart, it is not monastic or reclusive. There are obvious and open manifestations of true religion and the Lord's disciple makes no effort to hide his life from others, but it is not to receive honor from them that he does it. His concern for the poor and unfortunate is simply an extension of the compassionate love of his Father.

"But when you do a charitable deed, do not let your left hand know what your right hand is doing" (Matt 6.3). Not announcing our good deeds to others attacks the problem but incompletely. As the fourth-century writer and preacher Chysostom observed, "You may do good deeds before men, and yet seek not human praise; you may do them in secret, and yet in your heart wish that they may become known to gain that praise." It is for this reason that Jesus gives the second charge—don't announce it to yourself! That is the thrust of the Lord's metaphor about the hands. Our giving must be wholly unselfconscious—without any thought of some credit which will accrue to our account with others. We are not to keep the account (Matt 25.37). God will do that.

There is nothing which more poisons the stream of true goodness for others while we seek our own ends in every act of kindness. It costs its practitioner all sense of integrity, wholeness and peace of mind, not to speak of all reward from God. But remember that such hypocrisy is subtle, capturing our hearts when we least intend or expect it.

The greatest example of this heedless, uncalculating God-conscious mind is Jesus. His passion was never for Himself. He came into history wholly for the sake of others. He became flesh not to fulfill His own agenda, but to accomplish His Father's works (John 5.19), to speak His Father's words (John 7.16–18; 12.49–50) and to do His Father's will (John 5.30; 6.38; 14.31). It is just such a self-emptying spirit which every true disciple of the Lord longs after. It is, when practiced, the absolute death of all hypocrisy and sham. In the heart where Christ and His love for man sit enthroned there is no room left for self.

Take thought. Whenever you are acting to relieve the needs of the deprived and unfortunate and some sense of self-satisfaction and smugness begins to creep over you, or a longing for others to know just how noble you are—listen, and you will hear the sound of trumpets blaring.

Purifying Our Prayers

"**And when you pray, you shall not be like the hypocrites. For they love to pray standing in the synagogues and on the corners of the streets, that they may be seen by men**" (Matt 6.5). Jesus now takes up His second illustration of that selfless piety which is wholly God-centered and without guile. As in the case of almsgiving He plays it off against the known practice of the religious hypocrites.

Prayer is not a spiritual option. It rests at the essential center of man's relationship to God; true righteousness and prayer are inseparable. That is the reason that there is nothing more profane than playing to the galleries when one is supposed to be addressing God. It is a daring kind of contempt hurled directly into the face of the Majesty on high. It is bad enough to play hypocritical games with the poor. It is disastrous to dissemble in God's face.

Prayer by its very nature requires the opening of the heart in utter simplicity to the Almighty. This spirit is never better expressed than in the appeal of David: "Search me, O God, and know my heart; try me, and know my anxieties; and see if there is any wicked way in me, and lead me in the way everlasting" (Psa 139.23–24). When we put even our conversations with the Ruler of the universe into the service of an arrogant vainglory we have made considerable advance in the art of spiritual corruption.

Kingdom citizens, says Jesus, are not to pray like the hypocrites of the synagogue. The Pharisees and their ilk loved to pray, but they did not love God. Jesus once borrowed the words of Isaiah to describe them: "These people ... honor Me with their lips, but their heart is far from Me" (Matt 15.8). Their crime was not in mere indifference to God. They could have accomplished that by not praying at all. These humbugs were using prayer as an instrument of self-elevation, a means of establishing a cheap reputation for piety.

The Lord in this instance is not issuing an attack on public prayer. As earlier noted, the sin of the scribes and Pharisees was not in being seen, but in their *desire* to be seen. They loved to pray, not for the love of prayer or the God they were addressing, but for the love of themselves and the occasion it gave them to put their "piety" on parade. The style of the Pharisees' prayers was like that described in a newspaper account of a religious service which, with reference to the prayer, said, "The finest prayer ever offered to a Boston congregation!"

The sin of the hypocrites was not in standing to pray (a common practice among the Jews, Luke 18.13) or in doing so on a street corner or in the synagogue. Prayer played an important role in Jewish religious life, in Temple worship, in the synagogue and other public places, and in private personal devotions. Some of these prayers were fixed by tradition to certain times of the day (Acts 3.1; 10.30) and might be observed either publicly or privately depending on one's circumstances. The scribes and Pharisees, due to their love for celebrity (Matt 23.6; Mark 12.39), would likely have made sure that the hour of prayer found them on a major intersection. Private prayer would have held no charm for them.

"But you, when you pray, go into your room, and when you have shut your door, pray to your Father who is in the secret place; and your Father who sees in secret will reward you openly" (Matt 6.6). In order to make the thrust of His exhortation more intense, Jesus moves from the plural personal pronoun to the singular. He is wrestling here with a private, personal inner attitude and not with the forms of collective worship. Our true attitude toward God is far more revealed by solitary devotions than by public ones. Yet, as surely as Jesus does not by these words forbid public prayer, He is not simply urging His hearers to be diligent in private petitions. He is certainly not merely appealing to them to find a place to speak with God where there were minimal distractions of sight and sound. The "closet" or "inner room" in this passage is wholly figurative. The greatest distraction to true converse with God is not noise or other people but the human ego.

It is from this self-seeking mind that we must hide ourselves in order to pray to our Father acceptably. There is no physical hideaway which can secure us against pride. It attacks us everywhere, even in our "closets" where we can be found wishing even in our solitude that there was somebody there to appreciate our prayers. And later we can satisfy our wish by telling others how long and often we have prayed alone.

Our prayers to God can never be pure in any place until they become the artless expression of a self-forgetting mind caught up in the desire to honor and to please the One from whom all blessings flow. Pray always (1 Thes 5.17) and everywhere (1 Tim 2.8). Pray in the assembly of the saints and pray beside the bed. Pray amidst the bustle of the crowd or in a quiet retreat. Only be sure that your heart is genuine and your mind is true, that you speak to God and not to men. Otherwise, you will have been "paid in full" for your vanity (Matt 6.5b)—and it is a poor reward indeed!

Rote Does Not Make Right

"And when you pray, do not use vain repetitions as the heathen do. For they think that they will be heard for their many words. Therefore do not be like them. For your Father knows the things you have need of before you ask Him" (Matt 6.7–8). That there was a proclivity for long and pretentious prayers among Jewish scribes cannot be doubted. The author of the apocryphal book Ecclesiasticus (written in the intertestamental period) urged his readers that they "make not much babbling" when praying. Jesus excoriated the scribes of His time whose public prayers grew longer and more pretentious as their private lives grew more reprehensible (Mark 12.40; Luke 20.47). Even on the pagan side, Seneca spoke of those of his contemporaries who were guilty of "fatiguing the gods" with their interminable petitions.

We might be tempted to believe (given the emphasis of the preceding verses, Matt 6.2–6) that it is to this kind of hypocritical posturing in prayer that Jesus refers, save for the clear words of our text. There is an obvious shift at verse seven. Instead of the hypocrisy of the Pharisees, Jesus turns to reprove the ignorance of the Gentiles. Unlike the Jewish hypocrites whose only concern was for the acclaim of the crowd, these Gentile petitioners actually *wanted* to be heard by the powers of the heavens (Matt 6.7b) but were hindered in their efforts by a fatal ignorance of the real nature of God (note Acts 17.22–23).

Pagan prayers were born of the nature of pagan deities. The gods of Greece and Rome bore no resemblance to Jehovah of Hosts. They were morally indifferent, capricious and unpredictable, largely unconcerned with the affairs of men (note 1 Kgs 18.27). In most respects the Gentiles lived in terror of their gods and sought to placate or gain their attention by the endless repetition of ritual formulas. These incantations were thought to have a power wholly apart from the attitude or character of the petitioner. The pagan worshiper could rest no hope for a hearing on either the gods' sense of justice or their compassionate concern since they were devoid of both. Everything depended on the correctness of the formulas. Historian Will Durant described the Greek religion as "a system of magic rather than of ethics" (*The Story of Civilization*, Vol. II, p 201). Of Roman religion he wrote: "Did this religion help Roman morals? In some ways it was immoral: its stress on ritual suggested that the gods rewarded not goodness but gifts and formulas" (*The Story of Civilization*, Vol. III, p 67).

The key to prayer for the Gentiles was not in the earnestness of their spirits or in the godliness of their lives, but in "many words." The "*vain* repetitions" which Jesus rejects do not refer primarily to mere verbosity, and certainly not to earnest importunity in prayer which Jesus both exemplified (Matt 26.36–46) and commanded (Luke 18.1–8), but to a belief that the secret of effective prayer is in the words rather than in the life and attitude of the worshiper. Mindless repetitions do not engage the heart, and the heart is absolutely critical to communication with God (John 4.24). We must come to Him with a single-minded devotion.

The principle which Jesus sets forth there is violated today when we begin to think that the sheer number of our prayers is more important that the spirit we bring to them, or that the secret of their power is in their correct formulation. God is not a machine. It seems to me that there is a bit of this present in our mechanical insistence that a prayer is not acceptable unless it is concluded with the words, "in Jesus' name" or their equivalent. It goes without saying that we need to continually acknowledge and be aware of the impossibility of access to God save by the intercession of His Son. It is also edifying to remind ourselves even in our prayers that Jesus is our mediator with the Father, but "in Jesus' name" is not a magical formula calculated to guarantee God's acceptance of our prayer willy-nilly. As in the case of baptism "in the name of Jesus Christ" (Acts 2.38) or doing "all in the name of the Lord Jesus" (Col 3.17), it is something you *do*, not just something you *say*. To pray "in Jesus' name" (John 14.13) has some important implications for our attitude and behavior. It is to pray with a keen awareness of our Lord's redemptive mediation (John 14.6). It is also to pray with a spirit of submission to His will, a spirit unwilling to ask for anything which is contrary to His nature and eternal purpose (1 John 3.22; 5.14). Our carnal bleatings in God's direction will not be sanctified because we end our prayer with the expected "in Jesus' name" (Jas 4.3) any more than a "baptism" performed contrary to the Lord's instructions will somehow be made holy because someone pronounces that it is being done "in the name of Jesus Christ." Our absent-minded recital of prayer "words," however rich in content or beautiful of expression, will not open heaven's doors to us simply because they possess the right "form." Prayer in the kingdom of heaven is simply the earnest and open, yet reverent, conversation of a child with his Father—a Father he knows is eager and glad to hear him.

"Your Father Knows..."

The Gentiles spent most of their efforts in prayer just trying to get the attention of their unheeding deities. They also felt the need to inform their preoccupied gods of matters which might otherwise go unknown or unnoticed. Such concerns should never burden the prayers of Christians because, as Jesus says, **"Your Father knows the things you have need of before you ask Him"** (Matt 6.8). The true God is neither ignorant of His children's needs (so that we must inform Him) nor disinclined to provide them (so that we must persuade Him). He not only knows our needs absolutely and intimately but is profoundly concerned to supply them (2 Cor 9.8; 1 Pet 5.6–7; Eph 3.20). By this admonition the Lord seeks to remove from the hearts of His disciples that spirit of dread, fear and uncertainty which so ruled the prayers of the pagans. Kingdom citizens have a *Father* to whom they may always come with boldness and confidence (Heb 4.16; 10.19–22).

In giving assurance to His disciples of the nearness and approachability of the Father, Jesus has no intention of raising questions about the necessity of prayer. On the contrary, He means to make our lives even more prayerful. Prayer is seen as vital to life in the kingdom. Our Savior's own life was filled with earnest entreaties to His Father, and in this sermon He not only presumes that His disciples will pray but makes clear that in God's kingdom things not sought and asked for will be things not found (Matt 7.7–8).

Still, even conscientious minds are sometimes made to wonder. If God knows what we need and wants to give it, why doesn't He simply provide it without our asking? Doesn't this make the command to pray rather arbitrary and risk leaving the impression that God just enjoys seeing us grovel for our needs? One of the truths about God's nature which shines through the whole of Scripture is that He is never arbitrary or capricious in what He asks men to do (1 John 5.3). Every command has a purpose and is "for our good always" (Deut 6.24; 10.12–13). There may be a great deal about the purpose and working of prayer that we do not fully understand and have to receive by faith (I freely confess it on my own part) but there is enough light shining in God's word to help us see why there are some things which our Father cannot give us unless we ask for them.

Prayer is seen in Scripture as a function of faith and an expression of the heart (Matt 21.23; Rom 10.1). In our requests as well as in our praise we bend our wills gladly to His and declare that what He wants for us is what we want for ourselves. God may indeed know what we need and be disposed to give it but be unable to do so because of our lack of single-hearted faith (Jas 1.5–8). That is certainly true of the most precious treasures of the kingdom, the things we truly and ultimately need—love, joy, peace, godliness, holiness, kindness, goodness—all those marks of the divine nature which show that we are being conformed to the image of His Son (Rom 8.29). It is true that there are physical needs like food and shelter which God might provide without our request or our gratitude (Matt 5.45; Acts 14.16–17), but He seems intent even here on enlarging our willing trust in Him (Matt 6.11 with Deut 8.2–3). Perhaps He deals so with us in lesser matters because He knows that our lasting needs cannot be given to us without the yielding resolve of our own minds. Prayer is at its essence the opening of one's heart to God, inviting Him to act redemptively in our lives. In the divine scheme of things He cannot compel, but only moves within our personalities as we grant him the freedom to do so. God in His power can know the innermost thoughts of every person, good or evil, whether they will it or not (Heb 4.13; 1 Cor 4.5), but the cleansing and redirecting of those thoughts is not possible until their owner earnestly desires that his heart be so searched out as to remove every evil way (Psa 139.23–24).

For the wicked it is a source of dread to realize that God knows the secrets of the heart, but for the earnest, yielding, trusting soul such truth is the source of inexpressible solace. The thought that

God cares enough to take notice of what we do and what we think is both humbling and consoling. And to such a One as has so carefully and lovingly marked our way (Psa 139.1f) and so perfectly knows our needs we open up our hearts in utter faith: "Search me, O God, and know my heart; try me, and know my anxieties; and see if there is any wicked way in me, and lead me in the way everlasting" (Psa 139.23–24). It is just this kind of attitude in prayer that moves the hand of God by giving Him the freedom to do in our lives what He has always wanted to do and to give us what He has always wanted to give.

But if the spirit of faith in our prayers enables God to grant us what He wills to give, He is not limited by the content of our prayers. We often do not know how to pray as we ought (Rom 8.26–28) and in our ignorance ask for circumstances which would not work out for our good. Our loving Father will give us bread even when in our innocence we may be asking for a stone (Matt 7.9–11), and this is true because He "is able to do exceedingly abundantly above all that we ask or think" (Eph 3.20). What a blessing it is to pray to a God like that.

The Prayer that
Teaches Us How to Pray

Jesus has drawn three contrasts (Matt 6.2–3, 5–6, 7–8) when we come to Matthew 6.9–15. These verses represent the positive counsel which our Lord sets over against the mechanical prayers of the pagans. The Pharisees, He tells us, pray hypocritically, and the Gentiles pray mindlessly, but God's true people pray with an earnest, wholehearted devotion to Him and to His purpose in the world.

This brief prayer has come to be traditionally identified as "The Lord's Prayer." It is not the Lord's prayer if we mean that designation to suggest that He offered these petitions Himself. It is obvious that the sinless Christ could not have joined in an appeal to "forgive us our debts." It is also not the Lord's prayer in the sense that it is the only prayer whose words have His approval and which, therefore, has special acceptability. There is no evidence in all the New Testament that this brief petition was ever used as a liturgy. The apostle Paul filled his letters with prayer but his fervent petitions were never shaped to the form of the Lord's model, though they were certainly much influenced by its spirit.

The prayer that Jesus proposes for kingdom citizens is intended to be an example, a teaching model. Pray "in this *manner*," He said. Those who turn it into a ritual, a liturgy, and judge its power to rest in the correctness of its formulation have perverted it into the very kind of mindless incantation which the Teacher so vehemently abhorred. There is no magic in repeating it, but there is power in understanding it. Within its simple phrases we may learn the things which should be the burden of our lives as well as our prayers.

An obsession with things occupied the thinking and prayers

of the Gentiles (Matt 6.25, 32) but the children of the kingdom were in search of God and His righteousness. This fact is revealed in the initial section of Jesus' model.

The prayer is addressed to **"Our Father in heaven,"** an expression which is used twenty times in Matthew as a title for God. Jesus heavily emphasizes throughout the sermon this close personal relationship of His disciples to a personal God (Matt 5.16, 45, 48; 6.1, 4, 6, 8, 9, 14, 15, 26, 32; 7.11, 21). Kingdom citizens are sons of God (Matt 5.45) and may address Him in a way that lays claim to the closest and most personal relationship of all (Rom 8.15; Gal 4.6). The divine Fatherhood of which Jesus speaks is not the broad universal relationship that all men have with Him in creation (Acts 17.28–29). This is a relationship *chosen* by faith, a relationship that reveals itself in the marked way those who choose it resemble their Father (Matt 5.8, 44–45, 48) and do His will (Matt 7.21). This is how prayer begins for the Christian—as a child addressing his father, with all the rights and privileges which that relationship suggests (Matt 7.11). Only those who have received the "gospel of the kingdom" are privileged to say "Our Father in heaven." But there is nothing narrowly exclusive about this family. The whole world is being invited into it (Matt 5.13–16). The choice is ours.

The petitions of the prayer open with God at the center of concern. **"Hallowed be Your name."** The "name" of God in this appeal refers, as in other places in the Scriptures, not to a particular word, but to the nature, character and personality of God (note the reciprocal use of person and name in Psalm 91.14 and John 1.12). To hallow the name of God means simply to hold Him in reverence—to place Him in that special high and holy place where He belongs as the God of all creation and the Father of our Lord Jesus Christ. Of course, He is already the holy God, and there is no means at our command to make Him holier. The concern of this petition is that men everywhere should acknowledge in their own hearts and lives what is manifestly true. Every child of this Father desires that every other heart should know Him and glorify Him. So our prayers are to begin, not with a concern for ourselves, but with a concern for the honor of our Father. Prayer should begin with praise.

This theme is continued in the petition **"Your kingdom come. Your will be done, on earth as it is in heaven."** We believe this double petition to be a case of parallelism—the same thing repeated in different words. The Greek word for kingdom *(basileia)* carries at its root the idea of sovereignty and rule, and only suggest by extension the attendant concepts of territory and subjects. This "kingdom" is the rule of heaven in the person of Jesus Christ and it comes not to nations or lands but to individuals who receive the will of God in their hearts. The kingdom of God was destined to come in the power of the crucified and resurrected Lord (Mark 9.1; Rom 1.4), but the concern of this petition, as in the former one, is not that power be given to Christ (that was inevitable) but that men would acknowledge and submit to that power gladly. So the prayer is extended but the concern remains the same—that God's name be exalted, that God's purposes be accomplished, that God's will be done among men. Our prayers need to be filled in a preeminent way with this very central and vital concern. It should be paramount in the mind of every child of God. Otherwise our prayers for other needs will be forever out of joint and out of place. This is one of the lessons of the model prayer.

God Is Concerned
about "Little Things," Too

The order of Jesus' model prayer makes clear that the glory of God and the accomplishing of His will in the world must always be at the heart of the life and thinking of the Christian. His prayers, like his life, should begin and end there. It is on just such a note that the section of the sermon which contains this instructive prayer concludes (Matt 6.33). Yet this does not preclude the bringing of our own needs and burdens to God's throne. This is made evident by the three (some say four) concluding requests of the prayer (Matt 6.11–13). These all center on basic human necessities.

"Give us this day our daily bread" (Matt 6.11). With these words the Lord makes a sudden shift from the exalted to the commonplace. The apparent discontinuity of it caused many of the ancient commentators to spiritualize the "bread," but there is nothing in the context to justify it. On the face of things it just seems that physical considerations should be left till last, after forgiveness and the strength to endure temptation. But that is not where Jesus put them (either here or in Luke 11.2–4). He certainly does not intend that physical necessities become life's overriding concern (Matt 6.19–32) but He is also not discounting their importance. The "Word" who became flesh understood from experience the bodily needs of men (Heb 2.18; 4.15) and demonstrated how seriously He took them in His compassion for the sick and hungry (Mark 1.40–41; Matt 15.32; 25.41–43). The inclusion of this brief petition demonstrates that there is no matter so small that we may not with confidence bring it to our Father. Paul urges this: "Be anxious for *nothing*, but in *everything* by prayer and supplication … let your requests be made know to God" (Phil 4.6). Peter says the same: "Casing *all* your care upon

Him, for He cares for you" (1 Pet 5.7). Once we have determined to do His will at all costs, we may speak freely to Him of all our needs from the least to the greatest.

This simple petition speaks not only of God's wide-ranging concern but of our own complete dependence on Him. "Bread" as here used likely stands for all of life's bodily needs—food, shelter, health, family, *etc.* In any case we cannot by our own unaided strength supply one of them. As Clovis Chappell once observed, we could no more create one loaf of bread than we could create the universe. "The earth is the Lord's, and all its fullness" (Psa 24.1). Hence we have no real choice but to trust God even at the most elemental level.

The English translation "daily bread" is somewhat of an educated guess since the Greek word for "daily" occurs nowhere else for certain in Greek literature. It may suggest bread for the day ahead or bread sufficient to sustain us. In either case Jesus teaches us to ask for no more than a day's supply. This is a tough assignment for people like ourselves who are inclined to fall to pieces without a lifetime provision in hand and fully insured. If we follow the Lord's counsel we will quit trusting in bread (John 6.25) and learn to lean wholly on God and His promises. Learning to live trustingly with what we have each day calls to mind God's manna experiment with Israel while they were in the wilderness. "He humbled you," wrote Moses, "allowed you to hunger, and fed you with manna...that He might make you know that man shall not live by bread alone; but man lives by every word that proceeds from the mouth of the Lord" (Deut 8.3). Jesus had used this passage once to great advantage (Matt 4.4). We can do the same.

However much, then, it might have seemed at first that this prayer for bread was prayer from a very low ground, it turns out to have a powerful spiritual benefit. It teaches us faith. And this is a prayer for the poor and the rich alike; for no matter how little or how much we have or how hard we struggle to obtain and keep it, God alone can secure it. If we will learn to trust Him, God's children can live serenely in the confidence once expressed by the aged David: "I have been young, and now am old; yet I have not seen the righteous forsaken, nor his descendants begging bread" (Psa 37.25). And if we learn this kind of trust about bread, it will free us to get about the things that are even more important.

The Things We Cannot Live Without

"**And forgive us our debts...**" (Matt 6.12). Having begun with a petition which deals with God's concern for us at the most elemental level, daily physical necessities Jesus includes two final petitions which are concerned with some absolute imperatives of spiritual life. The first is an appeal for forgiveness. If there is anything puzzling about the form this appeal takes it is the use of the word "debts." Our Lord's intended meaning is made clear by Luke's account of the model prayer which has "sins" instead of "debts" (Luke 11.4). Jesus is simply using a metaphor for our failure before God. We owed Him something as His creatures and His children which we did not pay, and now we are unable to pay. The request for pardon is present tense and speaks to present mercy rather than to the future time of judgment.

This simple appeal for forgiveness for one's sins as a need of the kingdom citizen bears testimony to the fact that becoming a Christian does not end our battle with sin or our need for grace. There must be a continuing and increasing sensitivity to sin and all things shameful and dishonorable. Some disciples leave me with a haunting sense of foreboding by their stubborn refusal to confess and seek forgiveness for even the most obvious wrongs. One wonders if they have ever experienced repentance or, having experienced it, laid it permanently aside as a one-time event. If we have never known a true change of heart toward God then we are still in our sins and all the rest is not wroth sawdust. Sin is not a one-time-only phenomenon for the Christian (1 John 1.7–9). Neither is repentance. That is the reason that it is a happy thought to know that God's mercy is also not a one-time-only opportunity, and that His grace is "greater than all my sins."

God is certainly concerned for our physical needs but we can survive the loss of "daily bread." Indeed, there is indication that we may be called upon to do so. Paul speaks of the hunger, thirst, cold, and nakedness which he suffered in the service of Christ (2 Cor 11.27). Even the lives of God's people are not beyond forfeit (Luke 21.16; Rev 6.9). But the loss we cannot sustain is that of divine mercy and strength. We can suffer the loss of all *things* but we cannot suffer the loss of *God*.

"...as we forgive our debtors" (Matt 6.12b). Jesus adds this codicil to the appeal for forgiveness. The tense of the verb here speaks of what has been going on in the past right up to the present. It is interesting to note that people who are implacable and difficult to entreat are generally people who find it almost impossible to confess and renounce their own wrongs. Those who refuse mercy to others evidently demonstrate to God a total lack of that spirit of humble penitence necessary to obtain divine forgiveness (Matt 6.14–15; 5.7). This is powerfully expressed in the parable of the steward who was forgiven the unbelievable amount of $10 million and went out and ruthlessly seized by the throat a fellow who owed him $17 (Matt 18.21–35).

"And do not lead us into temptation..." (Matt 6.13). This petition reflects the desire of the forgiven man to live a new life by conquering the weaknesses which formerly brought him down. God intends that His people not only be forgiven but also transformed. "Tempt" and "temptation" in the New Testament are translations in each case of virtually the same Greek word *(peirazo; peirasmos)*. It means to try or put to the test. These trials may come from God Himself and be intended for the good of His children (Jas 1.2). Our faith may be tested by a hard commandment (Heb 11.17). Temptation or trial can come through persecution (1 Pet 4.12) which obviously has its origin with Satan but may be used by God to purify our faith (1 Pet 1.6–7). Physical suffering, grief and calamity can be the source of trial as was true in the case of Job. Satan was the source of Job's troubles but God used them to benefit His servant. Such was also the case of Paul and his thorn in the flesh (2 Cor 12.7). But the classic understanding of temptation and, I believe, the one now under consideration, is temptation to evil. These are the temptations being referred to in James 1.12–14 where the author is at pains to explain that such temptations do not come from God. The temptations from which the petition of the model prayer seeks deliverance have to do with "evil" or "the evil one" (Matt 6.13b).

Why should we seek help from God in the matter of temptations that arise from our own lusts and the machinations of the Devil? Because our Father has absolute control of the Tempter who cannot function without His permission (Job 1.10–12; 2.3–6), and because He has promised to provide strength by which we may "endure" temptation (1 Cor 10.13).

Is this a request to escape temptation altogether? This is inconceivable in view of such passages as 1 Corinthians 10.13; Hebrews 4.15; *et al.* What is far more likely as evidenced by the parallel appeal to be delivered from the evil one, is that this is an entreaty to be saved from the temptation's power so that we are not overwhelmed and caused to fall because of it. So, in our time of severe temptation, let us rush headlong to our Father that "we may obtain mercy and find grace to help in time of need" (Heb 4.6).

The Christian and Fasting

"Moreover, when you fast, do not be like the hypocrites..." (Matt 6.16). With these words Jesus begins the last of His three examples of true piety as contrasted with the empty posturing of the scribes and Pharisees. If we have mastered the lessons taught in the first two cases there are no great surprises in this third study. His hearers are again called on to direct their hearts toward God and away from themselves. This time the vehicle of His message is fasting.

Fasting was an established part of Old Testament worship. There was only one ordained public fast—the Day of Atonement (Lev 16.29–31)—but in times of special crisis both the nation as a whole (2 Chron 20.3; Ezra 8.21; Neh 9.1) and individuals fasted (2 Sam 12.16; Neh 1.4; Psa 35.13; 69.10). In the years of the captivity some new fasts were evidently added to commemorate the calamities which befell the nation at the hands of the Babylonians (Zech 8.19). By Jesus' day, the Pharisees had turned private fasting into a hard and fast twice-weekly routine (Luke 18.12).

The practice of fasting in Israel had a spiritual purpose. This abstinence from food for brief periods (usually a day) was never intended to be ascetic or therapeutic. It was simply a means of humbling the spirit before God in times of great distress (Psa 69.10) and had an almost inseparable link with prayer (Jer 14.12). Fasting was an expression of sorrow and was referred to as "afflicting" the soul (Isa 58.5). It was therefore frequently accompanied in the Old Testament with the customary signs of mourning—the wearing of sackcloth and covering oneself with dust and ashes (Neh 9.1; Est 4.1; Dan 9.3).

Unfortunately, even the fast of the Day of Atonement which was intended to be a national expression of humble contrition for Israel's sins often became no more than an empty ritual. "Indeed,"

God said through Isaiah, "you fast for strife and debate. ...You fast not as you do this day, to make your voice heard on high" (Isa 58.4). Old Testament history virtually closes with the Lord's grieved question to His people: "When you fasted and mourned... did you really fast for Me—for Me?" (Zech 7.5).

It was in the spirit of the Hebrew prophets that Jesus scored the mindless fasting of the Pharisees. Their puerile histrionics, the sad face, the neglected hygiene, were all for effect—to **"appear to men to be fasting"** (Matt 6.16, 18). The sin of "the hypocrites" was not in the sadness of their faces or their unkempt appearance. Such behavior might naturally characterize the genuine penitent who was held captive to the distress of his soul. Their sin was not in the fact that others learned they were fasting. Jesus had already made clear that God may be glorified when others see our good works (Matt 5.16). The disaster occurs when we do our good works to find glory for ourselves. It is not public worship which He reproves but worship for publicity.

The point Jesus makes in His third illustration of true Godward piety is eminently clear but the subject of fasting itself has been the source of questions. Did the Lord intend to ordain fasting for kingdom citizens or was He simply speaking to His Jewish followers in terms they could understand (*e.g.*, "gift to the altar," Matt 5.23–24)? He was once criticized for His feasting ways and His disciples' failure to fast as did the Pharisees and disciples of John (Mark 2.18–22). His reply was that for His disciples to fast while He was still with them would be as inappropriate as mourning at a wedding. Later, He said, when He was taken from them, their sorrow would turn them to fasting. All this tells us that the disciples of Jesus did not practice fasting as a matter of regular devotion. It also tells us that Jesus saw fasting as the natural expression of sorrow and deep concern and found it inappropriate for a time of joy. His announcement that His disciples would fast when He was taken away should be understood, not as a command, but as a recognition of the grief that was to come. Even this cannot be made to describe the whole Messianic period. In that time God promised that their fasts would be turned into joyful feasts (Zech 8.19).

What is evident as we wrestle with the Christian's relationship to fasting is that Jesus did not institute any fast days for the church, either public or private. There is also no indication that He ordained fasting as a matter of regular devotion. What He taught was that there will be times of deep concern when fasting will be a natural companion of our prayers. This seems to be exactly what was practiced in the church at Antioch and by Paul and Barnabas (Acts 13.3; 14.23) and should be our guide today.

The natural activism of the western mind has caused us to spend too little time in prayer and simple contemplation of God and His word. Our labors would likely be far more fruitful if we spent more time in meditation and thoughtful prayer before taking up our work. And if the critical nature of our petitions should move us to humble ourselves before God and set our hearts wholly upon Him by fasting, nothing untoward will have happened. Our Savior's only concern is that we worship God for Himself alone and not for prideful ostentation.

The Committed Heart

With Matthew 6.19–24 Jesus outlines His theme of the Christian's absolute love of God but from a new direction. The first and fundamental threat to that love arises from self—the pride and arrogance which corrupt all our attempts at piety (Matt 6.1–18). Following closely upon the problem of ego is the challenge of "the world"—not the universe, or the people in it, but the "world" as a mindset, a system of values, a way of looking at life that treasures the present and the tangible above everything (Luke 12.15).

This section of the sermon is a call to unreserved commitment in the choice between earth and heaven. Jesus begins by demonstrating why that commitment ought to be made to God and continues with two illustrations calculated to show the wretchedness and impossibility of trying to "ride the fence."

"Do not lay up for yourselves treasures on earth..." Jesus' warning about earthly treasures must not be trivialized into a prohibition of bank accounts or the mere possession of anything material. This admonition does not address the question of how much of this world's goods the kingdom citizen ought to possess but is concerned with his attitude toward them. The "treasures" of this text are understood to be whatever a man puts his whole heart into. They are not just things we value but things we value above all else. Our treasures and our persons become one.

Jesus' observations about the temporariness and uncertainty of such things as clothing, food and money constituted no news to His hearers. The world of our Lord's day was even more visibly fragile than our own. In their simple living conditions rot and mildew, insect and worm attacked their storehouses with a vengeance and their mud-brick walls offered no deterrent to thieves who could wipe out a lifetime overnight. Our modern refrigeration, closely guarded banks and casualty insurance often cause us to feel safely removed from the impermanence of the ancient world—but we should all know better. All "things" are subject to ultimate decay, the genius of man notwithstanding. It is impossible to secure material wealth against the ravages of time and circumstance. It is removed from us or we are separated from it (Ecc 6.13–15; Luke 12.20), and if we had it forever it would not bring us lasting satisfaction (Ecc 5.9–10; 6.7). Jesus means to protect us from the horror of seeing our whole lives go up in smoke (2 Pet 3.10).

It doesn't take much intellect to see that to rest one's very soul on such insubstantial vapor is an act of folly, but we must never underestimate the power of covetousness to turn our common sense into quivering jelly. We are living in an age which values men by the wealth they collect. It is madness, of course, but this spirit can breathe itself into us before we know it and suddenly we find ourselves mindlessly grubbing for "things" like all the rest. Materialism is destroying many disciples, some even while they are faithfully "going to church." The charade continues but their heart is no longer in it. Prosperity has become the trial of those of us who live in what is perhaps the richest society in human history, and it is severe. Thomas Carlyle once observed that for every ten men who can stand adversity there is one that can stand prosperity.

"...but lay up for yourselves treasures in heaven." This is not an exhortation to find a way to transfer the things we treasure on earth to a heavenly bank. If so, there is no information given about how to accomplish it. I once heard of a man whose love for his house and land, together with his premillennial speculations, moved him to seek a means of guaranteeing the return of his property when the Lord came to establish His kingdom on the earth. The treasures of heaven are altogether of a different kind than those we might store up here.

Jesus' message is a simple one: "Learn to cherish the things of heaven, the things that have to do with your Father. Only these will last." His call is not simply to a better and more lasting treasure but to a total allegiance, an absolute commitment. To have

one's treasure in heaven simply means to submit oneself completely to that which is *in heaven*—God's sovereign rule ("Your will
be done"). This is the theme that follows in the succeeding verses
(Matt 6.22–24). The key to understanding this whole section is
found in Matthew 6.21: **"Where your treasure is, there your
heart will be also."** The Lord is far more concerned with what a
man does with his heart than with what he does with his goods.
Things are not our problem. God created them. An appreciation
of things is not our problem. They have a God-given purpose. The
love of things is our problem (1 Tim 6.9–10)—the disposition to
let some moth-eaten old garbage take the place of the incorrupt-
ible God in our hearts.

The Single Mind

For each of us there is only one brief and fragile lifetime in which to choose the treasure which will fashion our eternity. It is a choice which calls for both sobriety and urgency. Jesus pleads with us to put our trust in the eternal God whose grace and power transcend time rather than the corruptible "things" which time destroys (see 1 Tim 6.17). This is exactly the thrust of Moses' observation in his farewell address to Israel: "He humbled you, allowed you to hunger, and fed you with manna ... that He might make you know that man shall not live by bread alone; but man lives by every word that proceeds from the mouth of the LORD" (Deut 8.3). The lifeless wealth of this world is but dust in the mouth, but to have a right relationship with God, that is the thing which makes a man truly rich.

It is a fatal flaw of the character to "*desire* to be rich"—whatever the reason (1 Tim 6.9). This is one of the symptoms of "thing-madness." It is not encouraging to hear some Christian say that he wants to obtain wealth in order to support gospel preachers or take care of the poor or do some other good work. The chances are very good that before those who need it see any of that longed-for money, his own soul will have been made captive to covetousness. Let him take with grateful contentment what God has given him already and use it in a selfless way. If a child of God ever becomes rich, may it never be because he planned it that way.

If we succeed in having our treasure in heaven, it will be because we have put our whole heart into the matter. There is no room for vacillation, indecision or lukewarmness in our attitude toward God and His kingdom. We must choose heaven and choose it unreservedly. As one writer observed, there is nothing more dangerous than trying to leap a chasm in two steps.

"The lamp of the body is the eye. If therefore your eye is good, your whole body will be full of light. But if your eye is bad, your whole body will be full of darkness" (Matt 6.22–23). Jesus continues His instruction on the Christian's battle to keep the world out of his heart with a simple illustration. He compares the function of the eye for the body with the influence of one's life-controlling perspective on the heart. The eye acts as the source of light for the body. A "good" (sound, healthy) eye fills the body with light. A "bad" (unsound, defective) eye leaves the body in darkness. The application comes in His concluding observation (Matt 6.23b): **"If therefore the light that is in you be darkness, how great is that darkness!"** As the eye is the window by which the whole body is either lighted or darkened depending on its condition, so the "eyes of your understanding" (Eph 1.18) determine whether the spirit of man is flooded with illumination or plunged into a Godless gloom. It is tragic enough to be physically blind, but when the spirit is denied true sight, how much deeper is that darkness of the soul! A single heart brings clarity and wholeness. A divided heart brings confusion and disarray. There is a sadness about the person who, forever uncommitted, goes through life in the unrelieved agony of his indecision. He never knows quite who he is or what he should do—no principles guide, no commitment governs—every fork in the road is a renewed trauma. How great is that darkness!

The "good" eye is a heart which hears the gospel with an utterly sincere simplicity. It is a mind which receives the gospel with an unqualified resolve. The spiritual vision is clouded by an unhealthy preoccupation with things. Materialism becomes the cataract of the mind. One reason so many people just cannot "see" the gospel or understand the Bible is because it does not fit their presuppositions about the importance of wealth. Christians who suddenly become confused and uncertain about the demands of kingdom life are often not so much experiencing an intellectual struggle as a spiritual one. The light of the gospel does not come to those whose loyalties are divided. As Jesus once observed, "If anyone wills to do His will, he shall know concerning the doc-

trine, whether it is from God or whether I speak on My own authority" (John 7.17). James says much the same thing in the practical exhortations of his very pointed epistle: "For he who doubts
is like a wave of the sea driven and tossed by the wind. For let not
that man suppose that he will receive anything from the Lord; he
is a double-minded man, unstable in all his ways" (Jas 1.6–8).

The blessings of the kingdom of God are not apportioned on
the basis of percentages—so many blessings for so much good
done. With Jesus it is either all or nothing. Either we give all and
receive everything, or we waver and vacillate and obtain nothing.
Those who successfully approach the kingdom of heaven must
learn the power and discipline of choosing "that good part" (Luke
10.42), doing the "one thing" (Phil 3.13), walking the "narrow"
way (Matt 7.13). This lesson is well expressed in the words of a
familiar hymn: "For we never can prove the delights of His love
until all on the altar we lay; for the favor He shows and the joy He
bestows are for those who will trust and obey."

The Impossibility
of Divided Loyalties

One of the less noted facts about the Pharisees is that they were "lovers of money" (Luke 16.14). Jesus related the parable of the Unrighteous Steward for their benefit, but they scoffed at its lesson. It should not be surprising then that a sermon that was in large measure addressed to the twisted and corrupting ways of the Pharisaic mind should contain a stiff warning about the dangers of too great an affection for things. Covetousness is subtle. It is just the kind of spiritual cancer which seems to live easily with a great display of piety. It does not have about it the open ugliness of gross immorality, yet this "respectable worldliness," through its subtlety, becomes even more dangerous.

"No one can serve two masters..." (Matt 6.24). To show the impossibility of attempting to "split the difference" between God and the world, Jesus employs the illustration of a man trying to serve two masters. The strength of His language will be better felt if we realize that the word translated "serve" is from the Greek *douleuein* which means "to be a slave to." The word translated "master" is *kurios* (often translated "lord") which suggest total ownership and control. A man simply could not be a slave to two owners, both demanding total service. The effort would result in satisfying neither master and making the life of the slave who tried it wretched. He would finally be forced by an impossible and intolerable situation to resolve his misery by choosing between them.

"Mammon" is from a common Aramaic word for wealth. It is so used both here and in Luke 16.9, 11, 13. Although it is in a measure personified by Jesus, there is no evidence for the existence of a Syrian deity by that name in New Testament times. The context dictates that the Lord is simply concerned with the love of money as a rival for true commitment to God. In Luke, the expression "unrighteous mammon" (Luke 16.9, 11) is used, likely signifying not so much that there was anything intrinsically evil about riches as that money and material possessions have been attended all too often by ungodly affections and behavior.

There is no such thing as a little covetousness. The love of things suffers no rivals and God will ultimately be forced out (1 John 2.15–17). For this reason it becomes dangerous to entertain in our heart any fascination with the wealth of this world. Materialism has a voracious appetite and will soon consume the personality which gives it an opening. Yet, when it finally rules without restraint, it brings no peace nor satisfaction—no lasting happiness. God also desires to have us exclusively for Himself, but for our benefit, not His. Money will consume us. He will fill us. Men who have been made for God will know no peace apart from Him.

The Greco-Roman world into which the gospel first came was a world where men were not called upon to choose between gods, but sought to serve as many as possible. There was always room in the Roman pantheon for another god or another mystery cult, and men were more concerned with serving too few gods than serving too many (Acts 17.22–23). None of their deities made any exclusive claim on their lives and the claims they made were more ritual than moral.

The only significant departure from the exceedingly accommodating religions of the ancient world was the religion of the Jews. The God of Abraham, Isaac and Jacob was relentlessly at war with all other deities, tolerating no rivals, demanding absolute loyalty (Exod 20.3–4; Deut 6.4–5). And it was this spirit and this challenge to radical and unequivocal choice that Jesus pressed in all His teaching and especially here in the Sermon on the Mount.

It ought not to surprise us that the God "who made the world and everything in it" should demand first place in our lives. What other place could the One from whom we draw our breath conceivably hold? It is beyond belief that the true and holy God would suffer Himself to be ranked in our hearts below mere lifeless mammon. Even our families must not rival Him (Matt 10.37) and, most significant of all, not even our very lives (Luke 14.26).

Mammon will cease to attract us so perniciously when we finally realize that riches have no independent power or reality—that even wealth, like all of creation, is ultimately traceable to the great and holy God. He is the One who "gives us richly all things to enjoy" (1 Tim 6.17) and fills our "hearts with food and gladness" (Acts 14.17). He is more than that. He is the giver of "every good gift and every perfect gift" (Jas 1.17). In Christ, "the fullness of the Godhead bodily," He has made us full (Col 2.9–10). Our fascination with money is just another case where we need to avoid the foolishness of the ancient Gentiles who "exchanged the truth of God for the lie, and worshiped and served the creature rather than the Creator, who is blessed forever" (Rom 1.25).

The Worldliness of Worry

Anxiety over things and circumstances is a foible we smile at. It seems such a creaturely thing to do—an exercise eminently human. But Jesus does not treat such anxiety lightly. Worry is seen from the divine perspective as a subtle but real form of worldliness and the Lord treats it under the heading of materialism. Some people aspire to wealth, while others are in terror of poverty. Both groups are equally occupied with things. In Matthew 6.25–34, Jesus warns His disciples that anxiety for things represents as great a threat to wholehearted devotion to God as covetousness (note Luke 12.13–31 where the Lord again associates the two). This is a fact with which most of us have been slow to deal. We have lived all too comfortably with regular bouts of hysteria over some suspected future deprivation. Our fears, as effectively as our passions, have been allowed to consume our energies, dominate our lives and steal away our hearts. Satan cares little as to whether we are consumed with greed or obsessed by worry as long as our minds are set on *things* rather than on God. The consequences of such worldly anxiety are not just spiritually regrettable, they can be fatal.

"Therefore I say to you, do not worry about your life, what you will eat or what you will drink" (Matt 6.25). Three times in this section of the sermon, Jesus commands His hearers not to be distressed and troubled over the things required to sustain this present life—food, drink and clothing (Matt 6.25, 31, 34). His warning, made all the more urgent by repetition, is intended to alert us to the real danger which an inordinate fretfulness over the "necessities of life" holds for us. The Lord's "therefore" in verse 25 makes clear that He is continuing to deal with the theme of *God vs. things*, and that the succeeding instructions rest upon the truth that men cannot serve God acceptably with a divided heart (Matt 6.24). For this reason, it becomes all the more interesting to note that the Greek word *(merimnate)* translated "do not worry" ("take no thought," KJV) is from a root *(meridzo)* which suggests being drawn in two directions; distracted; and, therefore, anxious, troubled. Luke uses this same word to report Jesus' description of Martha's state of mind when very much occupied with her duties in the kitchen (Luke 10.41), and Matthew uses it when record-ing the Lord's explanation of the thorny ground in the parable of the Sower as those whose lives have been choked by "the cares [*merimna*] of this world" (Matt 13.22). God and His will are in-evitably driven from the heart of those who live in constant fear that they may at any moment be deprived of life's necessities.

Still we must understand that, like His warning about storing up this world's goods, Jesus intends by His prohibition of anxiety to raise the question of where one's ultimate trust is to be placed and not to forbid a concerned effort to make a living. Working as a means of obtaining a livelihood is not just tolerated by the Scriptures, it is commanded (Eph 4.28), and sluggards are not treated gently (Prov 6.6–11; 24.30–34; Ecc 4.5). There is noth-ing spiritual about indolence. "If anyone will not work," wrote Paul, "neither shall he eat" (2 Thes 3.10). This warning, then, is not directed at the thoughtful concern of a conscientious husband or father to provide for the future needs of his family (1 Tim 5.8; 2 Cor 12.14). It is certainly not intended to disallow the burden of care the Christian feels for his brethren (1 Cor 12.25; 2 Cor 11.28; Phil 2.20) or for "the things of the Lord" (1 Cor 7.32). What the Lord strikes at here is the investing of one's primary concern in how to keep breathing and the mindless, fruitless fears associated with it.

That Jesus is primarily concerned with the choice between the world and the kingdom is made evident by the full context of His warning about worry. The thought that begins with "do not worry about your life" in verse 25 is not completed until verse 33: "but seek first the kingdom of God." This is the same "not … but" construction which the Lord used in John 6.27 when making the same point: "Do *not* labor for the food which perishes, *but* for the food which endures to everlasting life." Here, as in Matthew, the Great Teacher's intention is not to demand absolute abstention from one and the exclusive pursuit of the other. He is simply challenging us to decide which will hold the high ground in our hearts—food, drink and clothing or the righteousness of the rule of heaven—that which perishes, or that which abides. God must always be the first love of those who choose the latter.

So far in His sermon, Jesus has made it clear that we can lose eternity to greed, or we can forfeit it to anxious fear. Given the consequence of both, one road seems hardly less reprehensible than the other.

Lessons from the Birds and Flowers

In Matthew 6.25 Jesus issues His warning about a mindless anxiety over life's necessities—the brooding fear that God may not supply what we in our frailty cannot provide for ourselves. He follows His warning with a series of arguments which make clear that our incessant stewing over future needs and circumstances runs contrary to the very nature of God and His gospel and is consequently needless, useless, and insidiously destructive of faith (Matt 6.25–30).

That men are fragile and dependent creatures is not arguable. If we determine to face life on our own we have the greatest cause for anxiety—the rich as well as the poor. The twentieth century has not changed that. Neither wealth nor government programs are a defense against privation. Fortunes fail, governments fall, and circumstances change with disturbing regularity. Today's favorites are tomorrow's outcasts. It is therefore cause for no surprise that the world of unregenerate men is a quivering mass of anxious fear and trembling.

But what about those who are citizens in God's kingdom? Is it conceivable that they, too, should be racked by the same unrelenting fear of future calamity? And if so, what does this say about the certainty of God's promises or the constancy of His love? Christians should be the most positive and forward-looking people on earth. And this is not mere psychologizing—the baseless, sunny fluff of secularists trying to whistle their way past the graveyard. The optimism of Christians rests solidly on the love of God—a love already made marvelously manifest in the world. Jesus speaks of some of those evidences in His arguments against anxiety.

"Is not life more than food and the body more than clothing?" (Matt 6.25b). The word translated "life" (*psuche,* often translated "soul") refers here to the natural life of man rather than his higher spiritual nature. This is made evident by the parallel use of "body." The Lord begins at ground level with an argument from creation—an argument from the greater to the lesser. The very fact that we are alive at all, He says, reflects divine will. Why should the Creator give us life, only to starve us to death? If He gave us the greater gift of life, why would He withhold the lesser gifts necessary to maintain it? Can't we trust the One who gave us life to give us food? Our lives are not a fluke, and their continuation is not dependent on blind chance. We have been created in the image of God for purposes which He will surely work out by His faithful providence. What is our problem? We have forgotten the wonder of our origins and, therefore, fallen into skepticism about our future.

"Look at the birds of the air…" (Matt 6.26). **"Consider the lilies of the field…"** (Matt 6.28–30). In these two appeals, Jesus draws again on the nature of things, but now argues from the lesser to the greater. Look thoughtfully *(emblepsate)*, He urges, at the kind of rich provision which God makes for some of His humblest creatures, the birds, and ask yourselves how rich and full indeed will be His care for those who have not only been made in His image, but have become by His grace something even more remarkable—His children. Learn the lesson *(katamathete)* of the "lilies," He continues. Note how these wild, untended flowers of the field flourish by the sheer provision of God—and yet are more magnificently arrayed than Solomon on his grandest day. If God covers with such beauty the short-lived field grass, how do you suppose He will clothe those whose destiny is eternity? Why, then, Jesus asks, do we make our effort to gain life's provisions such an agonizing struggle—a struggle that winds up consuming our whole personality? And His answer is: because our faith is too small; because we have so little confidence in God (Matt 6.30).

"Which of you by worrying can add one cubit to his stature?" (Matt 6.27). In the midst of helping us see why our special relationship to God should give us great assurance of the future, the

Lord asks a question calculated to show the absolute absurdity and futility of being fretful over things we have no power to change. We need to do what we can. The birds are incapable of working the fields and the lilies of toiling at the spinning wheel, but we are able to make some contribution to our needs. There are limits, however, and it makes no sense for us to race our engines and strip our emotional gears when we have gone as far as we can go. Many times our fears are of imagined catastrophes, but even when the source of our dread is real, all our agitation avails nothing against the things we cannot change and serves only to incapacitate us of the good we might otherwise do. As in the case of the birds and the lilies, God will take care of what we cannot.

The question that needs to haunt us amidst our anxiety for the future is suggested in Paul's triumphant affirmation in Romans: "If God is for us, who can be against us? He who did not spare His own Son, but delivered Him up for us all, how shall He not with Him also freely give us all things?" (Rom 8.31–32). Do people who are ruled by anxious fear over what they are going to eat, drink, and wear really believe that Jesus died for their sins? **"O you of little faith."**

A Faith Too Small

Jesus, having made His reasoned appeal against worldly fears, repeats with urgency the warning with which He began, **"Therefore do not worry..."** (Matt 6.31). Then He adds one last telling observation.

"For after all these things the Gentiles seek" (Matt 6.32). Jesus' references to the "Gentiles" or "the nations" in the Sermon on the Mount do not so much speak to their race as to their spiritual ignorance—those who do not know God. Moving further in this direction, the apostles Paul, Peter and John, even when writing to disciples who were themselves non-Jews, refer to the unbelievers generally as "Gentiles" (1 Cor 5.1; 1 Thes 4.5; 1 Pet 2.12; 4.3; 3 John 7; Rev 11.2).

As He had done before (Matt 5.47; 6.7), Jesus chides His hearers with being no better in their behavior than the heathen. He does not describe the Gentiles as "worried" over food and clothing but says that they "seek" them. That the two expressions mean the same is evidenced by their interchangeable use in a similar teaching of the Lord in Luke 12.22, 29. By both terms, Jesus means not just "concern" but *ultimate* concern. The Gentiles in their darkness had food and clothing as their paramount interest. It dominated and controlled their lives. Knowing nothing of a gracious, benevolent God, they saw life as a matter of blind chance or unalterable fate. Their anxiety for things was altogether consistent with their world-view. What else was there? But that Christians should find no more peace of mind than those who were "without hope and without God in the world" was both unthinkable and shameful.

There is a sense in which all men, down to the most godless, are more important to the Almighty than birds and flowers, but

Jesus is not addressing them here. He is speaking only to those who are God's children, not merely in creation, but in redemption. And so He is saying, "You are God's very own people. How can you be so anxious and troubled?"

"Faith" in the kingdom of God is much more than a vague principle. It is an active, practical force which affects the whole of life. "Little faith" is a faith which has not been carefully thought out and applied. The Twelve in their relationship with Jesus is a story of the growth of a very small faith. Early on, as they first began to follow Him, they had freely and enthusiastically confessed Him to be the Christ, God's Son (John 1.41, 45, 49), but it is evident from later events that the implications of that fact had not fully dawned on them. This is dramatically illustrated by the terror which seized them when a sudden storm on the Sea of Galilee threatened to capsize their struggling vessel. They had been with Him now for more than a year. They had watched Him turn water into wine at Cana; seen Him return a dead son alive to his widowed mother's arms at Nain; experienced the miraculous catch of fish in the waters off Capernaum—but if they thought of such things amidst their wildly pitching boat, it did not serve to calm their rising panic. Think of it. The One who made heaven and earth is sleeping at their feet and they are afraid of drowning!

Afterward, when the Lord's mere word had calmed the storm, the Twelve were amazed. "Who can this be," they said, "that even the winds and the sea obey Him?" (Matt 8.23–27). He was just as they had confessed Him—the Son of God—but they were still learning what that meant. And so it is often with us. We have confessed that He is the Lord of glory, and we do in a measure believe it, but it has not yet come to influence our thinking about the totality of life. And so to us, as to them, He must reprovingly say, "O you of little faith."

But for what is our faith too small? That is the question. Too small to give us comfort in time of suffering? Too small to give us courage in the face of trial? Or, even more hauntingly, too small to save us in heaven? How small is that faith which lives in fearful anxiety over things? It must be small indeed, for Jesus once told His chastened disciples, "If you have faith as a mustard seed...nothing will be impossible for you" (Matt 17.20). The Lord's concern over our worrying ways is ultimate. He is not merely offering prudent counsel; He is issuing a command upon which our relationship to the kingdom of God hinges. Facing this fact honestly can serve at times to fill us with despair. We are so disposed to chronic fearfulness and, as much as we come to hate it, our struggle with our fears seems always to be more of a long, plodding war of attrition than a quick, decisive engagement. We share the anguish of the suffering father who, half-doubting, brought his tormented son to Jesus for healing. "I believe," he pled, "Help my unbelief" (Mark 9.24). It will help us if we realize that the freedom from fear to which Jesus calls us is a lesson we master over time, by long practice—by reminding ourselves again and again of what the cross says about the unchanging faithfulness of our Father's love and by prayerfully taking our burdened thoughts to Him (Phil 4.6). Finally, like our brother Paul before us, we will "learn the secret" (Phil 4.11–12) and be held in the unbreachable stronghold of the peace of God (Phil 4.7). "Be not anxious," He has said to us. In answer let us say, "We will not be anxious." Be strong and persevere. Remember. Faith can grow.

God Above All

"But seek first the kingdom of God and His righteousness" (Matt 6.33a). This concluding charge is the positive counterpart of Jesus' earlier warnings against a troubled and overweening concern for things (Matt 6.25, 28, 31). Now for the last time and in the clearest way the Son of God declares what must be the controlling passion of every Christian. There are no surprises in it for anyone who has been listening. The sentiment of this sentence represents the dominant theme of the sermon, a theme which has surfaced repeatedly (Matt 5.6, 16, 48; 6.20). The true servant of God must seek His kingdom and His righteousness above all else. It is God alone who deserves and commands our unreserved ambition and concern. It is in His kingdom that we should invest our hearts unconditionally. It is in His righteousness that we should expend our energies without stint. Here lies the key that unlocks all doors—the treasure that answers to all needs.

"The kingdom of God" in this text does not refer to the general sovereignty of God in creation and history, but to His specific rule over His redeemed people. Further, it does not refer so much to the people who submit to that rule (the church) as to the reign itself. To understand this weighty appeal as a call for absolute loyalty to the church as an institution would be a tragic misdirection. This is simply a summons for men to take the will of God as the supreme good.

Those whose millennial speculations cause them to see in Jesus' words a reference to some future apocalyptic kingdom have failed to see that the emphasis is not on what God will bring to pass in the future, but on what men must do in response to what God already has done and is doing. The Lord is making a call to present duty, not to mere passive anticipation. We do not question that the "kingdom" can encompass God's reign in His Son from the ascension to the judgment, but future events do not seem to be the Lord's principal concern in Matthew 6.33.

Since the kingdom in this passage has reference to the sovereign rule of God over His people, what we must "seek" is the submission of our wills to His. Every thought must be brought "into captivity to the obedience of Christ" (2 Cor 10.5). The emphasis, it seems to me, is not so much temporal ("look for the establishment of the kingdom") as moral ("prepare your heart to receive the rule of God's Anointed").

And why did Jesus add "and His righteousness?" Does this advance His thought or simply repeat it? There would seem to be little difference between the reign of God and the righteousness to which that reign calls all men. But some distinction may exist. The "righteousness" of the Sermon on the Mount is not justification by faith, though salvation by grace is implicit in the whole structure of the sermon. As context demonstrates, this "righteousness" is the righteousness of a changed life. It is the practical righteousness of a true love for others (Matt 5.20–48) and a single heart toward God (Matt 6.1–18). The kingdom of heaven intends to produce not only a new relationship with God, but a new and transformed life as well. The quest for that kingdom will not be a shallow or narrow one. It will profoundly affect every facet of our lives—marriage, home, family, profession, finances, lifestyle, _ad infinitum_. The Lord has taken us in His instruction to the marrow of the bone. As John R. W. Stott sums it up: "So just as Jesus has already called us in the Sermon to a greater righteousness, a wider love and a deeper piety, he now calls us to a higher ambition" (_Christian Counter-Culture_, p 169).

"…and all these things shall be added to you" (Matt 6.33b). While drawing His listeners to a loftier aspiration, Jesus does not dismiss the concern for food and shelter as without merit. He simply tells us that if we want assurance of "these things" we must quit seeking them and seek God. If we seek the present, we will lose both it and eternity. If we seek heaven, earth will be thrown in. We cannot pray for our daily bread until we have first sought God's glory and His will even more earnestly.

There is a very important principle involved in this relationship of bread and the kingdom. If we give ourselves absolutely to the pursuit of things it will serve to corrupt every other ambition. If, however, we seek first God's kingdom, all other aspirations are enhanced and ennobled because they are always made to serve a higher end. Life may seem to present us with an almost endless variety of options, but in the end there are only two. We either serve heaven or we serve ourselves. This exhausts the alternatives. The Sermon on the Mount is very clear about that.

Judgment Without Mercy

Most commentators have found Matthew 7.1–12 a challenging passage, difficult to fit into the fabric of the rest of the sermon. It appears at first examination to consist of three self-contained paragraphs without a common theme. This has caused some to assume that they were spoken on other occasions and arbitrarily included here. This is a needlessly radical solution which only serves to cast doubt on the accuracy of Matthew's reporting.

What these seemingly unrelated teachings may have in common is that they provide some needed caveats to balance Jesus' earlier instruction. If so, the tenor of the Lord's final cautionary words would be something like this:

Our own accurate understanding of kingdom righteousness should not produce in us a spirit of harsh, censorious judgment toward those who are having a struggle of it. Men need to be helped to see the nature of true righteousness, but not by an uncaring and self-righteous hypocrite who is more concerned with the sins of others than his own. If the sermon is first applied rigorously at home, we will easily find the compassion and humility to treat the sins of others (Matt 7.1–5).

The sharing of the gospel of the kingdom is an absolutely vital work, but we need to be warned not to waste our time on those who have no interest in it. The kingdom of God is not spread by an unheeding zealotry any more than a harsh judgmentalism. The child of the kingdom is looking for those whose attitude makes them ripe to receive the good news of redemption, not for men and women whose pride makes it impossible for them to hear and understand (Matt 7.6).

And, finally, the kingdom is not obtained by heroic endeavors and meritorious achievements, but simply by asking earnestly for it. The kingdom is a gift of God's love (Matt 7.7–12).

"Judge not, that you be not judged" (Matt 7.1–2). The Greek word *krinete,* here translated "judge," may carry in both Greek and English a wide range of meanings from *discernment* to *condemnation.* The context clearly points to the latter. Neither the exercise of a judicious discrimination (clearly required by Matt 7.6, 15–20) nor the existence of courts of law is being forbidden. It is a merciless condemnatory spirit which Jesus rejects. This is borne out by the parallel material in Luke where the warning against judging others is preceded by the positive, "Be merciful, just as your Father also is merciful" (Luke 6.36). In this admonition, Jesus returns to the theme of brotherly love which reached a climax in Matthew 5.43–48. In Luke's account of the sermon, the two sections are immediately joined (Luke 6.27–38). Our Lord's point is that people who are so much in need of mercy have no business being so merciless toward others. This warning is but the opposing face of His earlier promise that those who show mercy will receive mercy (Matt 5.7) and those who forgive will be forgiven (Matt 6.12). Those who condemn others without compassion or redemptive intent can expect the same treatment at the hands of God—a chilling prospect.

"And why do you look at the speck in your brother's eye, but do not consider the plank in your own eye?" (Matt 7.3–5). Because the kind of judging under consideration is loveless and self-seeking, it is often accompanied by hypocrisy. For this reason, Jesus paints the pathetically humorous picture of a man trying to extract a speck of dust from another's eye while a log is protruding from his own. Spiritually speaking, there are altogether too many blind eye-surgeons who are greatly exercised over the faults of others and oblivious to the enormity of their own. Fortunately, a serious attention to our own failures has the effect of equipping us with sufficient humility to deal patiently and skillfully with the sins of others (Gal 6.1–3; Tit 3.2–3).

The greatest practical difficulty which attaches itself to this very familiar set of verses is the popular idea that it virtually forbids all reproof, regardless of motive. The broad context of the

New Testament makes this understanding impossible. Jesus' teaching contains much rebuke (*e.g.*, Matt 23 and present text), yet it is never harsh or censorious. As the Lord Himself observed, "God did not send his Son into the world to condemn the world, but that the world through Him might be saved" (John 3.17). And that is the key. It is not loving, redemptive reproof which the Lord rejects here, but loveless attacks which serve only to feed the ego of the "judge."

The gospel of grace cannot be preached without convicting men of sin (John 16.8) and calling for a change of heart (Luke 24.47; Acts 2.38; 3.19; 17.30). Even the souls of God's redeemed people cannot be secured without admonishing the disorderly (1 Thes 5.14) and seeking to convert "a sinner from the error of his way" (Jas 5.19–20). But such correction is offered in redemptive love, not as the vehicle of pride and anger. The righteousness of the kingdom warns, but it does not attack. Citizens of God's kingdom, struggling with their sins and beset by weaknesses, need a brother—not a "judge." In all our dealings with others, we need to remember that we are not agents of the Lord's judgment, but of His salvation. Vengeance belongs to the Lord. Our task is to seek and to save the lost.

Of Pearls and Pigs

"Do not give what is holy to the dogs; nor cast your pearls before swine" (Matt 7.6). Given the emphasis in the preceding verses on compassion toward others' faults, the Lord's language here can seem a bit startling. It is not as though Jesus never used strong metaphors to describe the spiritual attitude of certain people. He referred to Herod Antipas as "that fox" (Luke 13.32) and to the Pharisees as "serpents, brood of vipers" (Matt 23.33). But this passage differs. No specific group of men is being addressed. "Dogs" and "swine" do not refer to the Gentiles or to a certain class of extraordinarily reprehensible sinners. They are simply figures in proverbial statements after the mold of 2 Peter 2.22. Both proverbs illustrate the futility of trying to offer something of great value to someone incapable of appreciating it. "What is holy" refers to the Old Testament sacrifices of which the priests alone could eat (Exod 29.33; Lev 2.3). The special significance of this sacred meat would be wholly lost on a cur dog (not the lap dogs of Matt 15.26–27) who would simply gulp it down with no more relish than if it were a piece of rotting garbage. In a similar way, it is pointless to try to teach swine the special value of pearls which any self-respecting pig would gladly tramp under foot to get to even the most repulsive of slop. No gratitude for such generosity should be expected from these sources. Their response may be more than indifferent; it may be violent.

How do these proverbs fit into the context of Jesus' earlier words about harsh judgment? They provide important balance. Even if fallible, sinful men are ill-equipped to sit in harsh judgment of their fellows, they are not therefore expected to view men with a naïve gullibility. In sending out the Twelve to teach, Jesus warned, "Behold, I send you out as sheep in the midst of wolves. Therefore be *wise as serpents* and harmless as doves" (Matt 10.16).

The Lord's caution was not cynical, only prudent. He wants His disciples to be utterly harmless in their relationship with others, but at the same time to recognize that all men "have not faith" and some will be stirred to animosity by the gospel.

What application does the Lord intend us to make from these proverbs which seem almost to stand apart from their context? Guelich feels that these are words of warning to the disciples against apostasy and the consequent loss of what is holy and precious (*The Sermon on the Mount*, pp 355–356). This seems unlikely, since it is the disciples themselves who are being called on not to offer holy and precious things to the uncaring. It is far more probable that Jesus is warning His followers not to press the gospel on uncaring and indifferent ears. His words are not intended to be disdainful or disparaging and do not apply to unbelievers as a class, but to those whose spirit makes them incapable of understanding the gospel (Rom 8.7; 1 Cor 2.14). Later, He gives much the same counsel to the Twelve, urging them to preach to "the worthy," but not to waste their time with those who will not hear them (Matt 10.11–14). Unhappy as it is, there are some people who, no matter how patiently taught, simply do not have "ears to hear" (Matt 11.15; 13.13–14).

There is an important lesson for us to learn in all this. We may have a special longing to teach and convert to Christ a certain person or group of persons. It may be a loved one or a special friend, or even a special class or nation of people. There is nothing wrong with such a deep longing for the salvation of others, but it must not blind us to their unconcern and indifference and the waste of effort which would be better spent on more receptive hearts. Patience is good, but we ought not go on pumping forever on an apparently dry hole. Other hearts are *longing* to hear. These are the ones we need to be searching out. It is a heartbreaking thing to be daily witness to the lost estate of your own children, parents, wife, husband, friends. What are we going to do when those we love are so unconcerned? The Lord is saying to us, "Go out and teach someone else's children, someone else's mother and father." Paul had this hard experience. He loved his nation with an unmitigated passion (Rom 9.1–3), but they had no "ears to hear." What was he to do? Still praying for his lost brethren in the flesh (Rom 10.1), he turned to invest his energies with those whose hearts were more receptive, the Gentiles (Acts 13.46–48; 18.6). They were not "his kind of people." They were morally corrupt, degraded, idolatrous; but they were willing to listen and to learn. When those in our own community, our own people, do not respond positively to the gospel, we need to seek out other communities, other people, and preach to them. The gospel, and time, are too precious to be wasted on those who do not care. The same might be said of preachers who work year after year with churches that show no interest in growing up in Christ or accomplishing His great work. These preachers need to leave these hopeless ruts and join their labor with disciples who, however backward now, are open and willing to learn and grow.

A Kingdom for the Asking

"**Ask, and it will be given to you...**" (Matt 7.7). There is something powerfully comforting about this final section (Matt 7.7–12) of the central body of our Lord's great sermon, but it is susceptible to serious misunderstanding. This invitation of Jesus is so memorable in itself, so easily carried in the heart like some grand all-encompassing assurance, that it has often been seen as the Aladdin's lamp of every human desire—the guarantee that if we pray for it, God will do it. That is not the case, and only by lifting this promise from its context could such a view of it be held.

Why does Jesus close His discussion of kingdom righteousness with these words of strong encouragement? If Matthew 7.1–5 is directed at those inclined to become kingdom Pharisees, this section is aimed at that far greater number who might despair before the demands of love. In their weakness and unworthiness, they see the lofty standards of the kingdom as unattainable. The Lord now makes clear that it is to just such hearts as long for righteousness out of a desperate necessity that the kingdom of heaven yields itself. It is not a kingdom for the deserving, but for the desiring—a kingdom for the asking.

"**For everyone who asks receives...**" (Matt 7.8). Whoever may be the person commanded to ask, and whatever may be the blessing he seeks, there can be no doubt from Jesus' words that God will grant it. There is absolute assurance about this. Six times in two verses, Jesus says so. But does this promise apply without condition to everyone, and are there no limits on what might be asked?

From the broad context of the sermon, it is evident that Jesus' "everyone" cannot be universal. He has already warned that neither the self-serving hypocrite or the mindless ritualist will receive any reward from the Father (Matt 6.1, 7). Just as certainly excluded is the double-minded man whose asking and seeking and knocking are sporadic, uncertain and half-hearted (Matt 6.22–24; Jas 1.5–8). The "everyone" of this promise clearly has reference to the humble-spirited and pure-hearted man of the beatitudes (Matt 5.3–12). There is a similar passage in Jeremiah: "Then you will call upon Me ... and I will listen to you. And you will seek Me and find Me, when you search for Me *with all your heart*" (Jer 29.12–13).

The object of the asking, seeking and knocking is left unstated in our text. Does this mean that any request that is truly and earnestly made by the kingdom citizen will be granted? Are there no limits here? It will help us to understand the true thrust of this passage if we remember the central concern of the sermon. As a continuing and unvarying theme, Jesus' exposition of the nature and ultimate worth of the kingdom of God has threaded itself through all the verses of Matthew 5 and 6, and, here in this passage, reaches a grand finale. The kingdom described and extolled is now offered to every humble and contrite heart. It is not just any request that the Lord invites His hearers to make with confidence, but a request for the blessings of the kingdom of heaven. Though prayer is treated in the sermon, it is not treated for its own sake merely, but in order to illustrate the totally God-conscious life and the importance of hallowing God and His will above all else (Matt 6.5–15). Support for this understanding is found in Luke's parallel account of the same teaching where "the Holy Spirit" (Luke 11.13) replaces Matthew's "good things" which the Father will give "to those who ask Him" (Matt 7.11). God knows that we have need of life's physical necessities (Matt 6.32) and encourages us to pray for them (Matt 6.11), but these are not the true treasures which have been the burden of this sermon. The "good things" of this text are spiritual.

"Or what man is there among you who, if his son asks for bread, will give him a stone? ...How much more will your Father who is in heaven give good things to those who ask Him!" (Matt 7.9, 11). The basis of our confidence in seeking the kingdom of heaven rests securely on God's desire and ability to give "good gifts" to

His children. Some of our prayers may not receive a positive reply because our Father in His grace and wisdom knows they will not be "good gifts." But our desire for the "bread of heaven" will be met. The "righteousness and peace and joy" of God's kingdom (Rom 14.17) are "good" without qualification, and it is the Father's will to grant them to everyone who seeks them with his whole heart. And, so far as our other longings go, there is a great security in knowing that if, in our innocence and genuineness of spirit ("for we do not know what we should pray for as we ought," Rom 8.26), we ask for a stone instead of bread, our Father will not grant it. The thought of being able to ask God for anything with the absolute assurance of receiving it would be a frightening one. Alec Motyer expresses it well: "If it were the case that whatever we ask, God was pledged to give, then I for one would never pray again, because I would not have sufficient confidence in my own wisdom to ask God for anything" (as quoted by John R. W. Stott in *Christian Counter-Culture*, p 187). There are few of us who have not lived long enough to thank our heavenly Father for prayers that went unanswered.

The Golden Rule

"Therefore, whatever you want men to do to you, do also to them, for this is the Law and the Prophets." It is appropriate that we pay some special attention to Matthew 7.12, if for no other reason than that it is one of the best-known verses in the Bible and, sadly enough, very little practiced by those who know it.

The "golden rule" has come to be identified in a unique way with Jesus, but the Lord here describes it as at the very heart of "the Law and the Prophets" (note Rom 13.9–10). Memorable as it is, this passage carves out no new ethical ground, but is simply a restatement of Leviticus 19.18: "You shall love your neighbor as yourself." But if the command to do to others what you would have them do to you is not unique to Jesus, there is certainly a special intensity He brings to it by the compelling example of His own love: "A new commandment I give to you, that you love one another; as I have loved you." (John 13.34).

Perhaps the first thing that needs to be noted about the "golden rule" is that it compels us to deal with others by beginning with ourselves. We are not to determine our treatment of other men by looking at them and asking what they deserve, but by starting with ourselves and asking what *we* would want and need. God's children are to draw on an innate sense of self-interest in order to treat others graciously and redemptively. How, we must ask, would we want to be treated if we were in the same circumstances that now confront our fellow? How well this simple rule of conduct cuts through our self-justifying subterfuges! Suddenly, to the humble heart, the way becomes remarkably clear.

But if this is so, why is it that more people do not practice this principle that would so obviously revolutionize the world? Basically, because most people are selfish and self-centered. Every effort to alter men by educating them to the "golden rule" has failed because the subjects of this restraining effort continue to be essentially selfish. Only when that old self-serving way is broken will men be freed to treat others the way they themselves wish to be treated.

How then are men to be released from their basic selfishness and freed to see others as they see themselves? By looking first at God. Our fascination with self can only end when we have become fascinated with God. Is not the greatest commandment of all, "You shall love the LORD your God with all your heart…" (Matt 22.36–39)? When an absolute love of God has driven out of us an absolute love of self, we will be set free to love others as we love ourselves. Until that happens, the kind of overweening self-love which drives most men will preclude our ever being able to look on the interests of others in the same way we look on our own. What this says is that only God can deliver us from ourselves and enable us to love others selflessly. "We love Him because He first loved us" (1 John 4.19). That is the precise reason that no man who has not looked into the face of a holy, loving God and been driven to his knees in humble gratitude can ever practice the rule that is golden.

This very fact most likely explains why Jesus raises again the matter of neighbor love in the context of Matthew 7. It can help us understand what the "therefore" of our text points back to. Lloyd-Jones feels that Matthew 7.12 is a return to the subject of judging others, and this may indeed be so, but it is difficult to treat 7.6–11 as nothing more than a parenthesis. It seems more probable that the Lord is grounding His instruction for the treatment of others in God's gracious treatment of His children (Matt 7.9–11). Our Father's mercy and generosity toward us has not been what we deserved, but what we desperately needed. Surely, then, those who have received such grace are called upon to deal with others, not on the basis of what they deserve, but what they need. So, Jesus closes the heart of His sermon as He began it—with an appeal for a true righteousness which reveals itself in a selfless love for men, a love which rests solidly on God's gracious love for us.

The Challenge to Choose

The body of our Lord's great mountain discourse is unmistakably concluded with Matthew 7.12. The radical and unconventional nature of the Kingdom, its citizens and its righteousness has been clearly and powerfully drawn (Matt 5.3–7.12). The remaining verses of the sermon (Matt 7.13–27) contain Jesus' appeal for His hearers' commitment.

This remarkable spiritual address, which gives definition to all true gospel preaching, was not meant merely to inform, but to persuade. The Sermon on the Mount speaks to the will as well as to the understanding. It is a call to radical choice. And the Great Preacher does not intend that we escape either Him or His message. He is saying, in effect: "My sermon is ended. Now you must decide what you will do about it. Consider carefully. Choose wisely. Life and death are in the direction you take."

What is obvious in all this is the fact that, all God's power notwithstanding, men can reject His will. His long and arduous redemptive labor issues finally not in an irresistible edict (Acts 7.51; Heb 10.29) but in an earnest invitation (Matt 11.28–30). Man is not a robot. His will, by God's design, is sacrosanct. Jesus can woo, but He cannot compel. So He teaches us patiently, and then He urgently entreats.

In making His closing appeal, the Lord speaks of only two alternatives: two gates, two kinds of fruit, two foundations. The choice may be difficult, but it is not complex. We must decide between the way of submission and trust and the way of rejection and rebellion. He urges His hearers to choose between these alternatives, considering not only their demands but their consequences. Where will this road take me? What kind of fruit will this tree produce? Will this house withstand the ultimate storm?

The exhortations of this final section of the sermon can be

divided into three units (Matt 7.13–14; 15–23; 24–27). Between two admonitions to choose wisely there is an inserted warning about the danger to wise choice presented by false teachers.

The Narrow Way

"Enter by the narrow gate; for wide is the gate and broad is the way that leads to destruction, and there are many who go in by it. Because narrow is the gate and difficult is the way which leads to life, and there are few who find it" (Matt 7.13–14). Here Jesus openly urges His hearers to choose the way that is hard and constricted and reject an easier and more comfortable course. He even makes it clear that the road ahead is as relentlessly demanding as the gate by which it is entered, and more than that, it may at times be a lonely way since most men will not find it to their liking. The Lord's remarkably honest invitation to the kingdom makes the carnal appeals and syrupy promises of some modern preachers utterly repugnant.

There is nothing surprising about this invitation. It is an invitation to enter a kingdom whose most salient feature has been the narrowness of its focus and the single-mindedness of its commitment (Matt 5.48; 6.19–24, 33). The narrow gate is the Lord's sovereign authority and the straitened way obedient submission to His will. Those who enter will find themselves no longer doing the expected, the traditional, the obvious thing. Following the Son of God, their lives will be as different as their destination.

Obviously there are many things which those who choose the kingdom's narrow road must leave behind. We will be abandoning the carefree crowd which never has to ask whether what they are doing is pleasing to God. Most importantly, we will be discarding our old self with its arrogant, willful and selfish way and surrendering mind and thought to a wiser and more gracious Ruler (Matt 16.24–25; 2 Cor 10.4–5). Only in this way will we ever become meek and merciful, poor in spirit and pure in heart, able to love our enemies and pray for them that persecute us.

But if the kingdom's narrow way constricts the willful spirit and self-serving mind, it does not straiten *love* (Phil 1.9;

Eph 3.17–19); it does not constrict *peace* (Phil 4.7); it does not dry up *joy* (1 Pet 1.8); it does not squeeze out *mercy* (Eph 2.4); it does not crush out *goodness* (2 Cor 9.8); it does not strangle *hope* (Rom 15.13). All these abound on the narrow road. The only thing which the strait gate strips from us is that wickedness which poisons and destroys us. Only the man who still loves that wickedness will feel pressed in and suffocated by the King's highway. Sin is the thief which has come to "steal, and kill and destroy," but the "Good Shepherd" has come that men may have "*life*, and ... have it more *abundantly*" (John 10.10).

Wrinkles on the Narrow Road

"**Beware of false prophets, who come to you in sheep's clothing, but inwardly they are ravenous wolves**" (Matt 7.15). For only the second time in the sermon Jesus begins His words with a sobering "beware" (Greek *proskete*). The first addresses a danger from within—hypocrisy (Matt 6.1). He speaks now of peril from without—false teachers. There are some natural assumptions which lie behind the Lord's urgent warning (John R. W. Stott, *Christian Counter-Culture*, p 197).

The first is that false prophets were not just a theoretical possibility, but a palpable and threatening reality. The Son of God is telling us that the kingdom of heaven must be sought out in a world where lies and deceptions concerning it will abound. There is nothing new in this. The Old Testament is replete with warnings about false prophets (Deut 13.1–3; 18.20–22; Jer 23.13–32; 27.9–10; 29.8–9; Ezek 13.1–23; 22.28; Mic 3.11; Zeph 3.4). Jesus, in the last week before His death, will sound one final alarm about the future appearance of pseudo-prophets and pseudo-Christs (Matt 24.5, 11, 24) and the New Testament epistles reveal that the world of the apostles was full of them (Acts 20.28–29; 2 Cor 11.1–4, 13–15; Gal 1.6–9; Col 2.8, 16–19; 2 Thes 2.8–12; 1 Tim 1.19–20; 4.1–2; 2 Tim 2.16–17; 4.3–4; Tit 1.10–11; 2 Pet 2.1–2; 1 John 2.18–23; 4.1–3; 2 John 9–11; Jude 3–4; Rev 2.15, 20–24).

It is evident from the New Testament that there has never been a time when Christians have not been locked in controversy with some form of false gospel. Those who want to serve the Lord, but be free of any burdensome concern with false teachers are simply hoping for the impossible. No one is going to hold securely to the narrow road without having some wrenching engagements with pseudo-disciples who attempt to subvert their faith. There are a number of Christians who yet hold to the myth that there was an idyllic time in the history of God's people when false teaching was unknown and peace and unity reigned supreme. For the security of our own faith, we need to drop that illusion and realize that "we must through many tribulations enter the kingdom of God" (Acts 14.22) and that some of those tribulations will arise from our own brethren who will speak "perverse things, to draw away the disciples after themselves" (Acts 20.30). Our Savior has given this warning from the outset. The greatest threat to those who are earnestly seeking to enter the strait gate is that gaggle of deceivers who always seem to be hovering around where issues of life and death are being deliberated. These false disciples are masters at making unclear what is eminently obvious—the difference between God's will and man's, the distinction between the broad and narrow way.

But who are these false prophets of whom Jesus speaks? They seem to be not only of the future, but of the present—teachers who were standing even then to prevent the entry of earnest souls into the kingdom of God. We think almost immediately of the scribes and Pharisees whose perversions and hypocrisy have been a dominant concern of this great sermon. It is true that they were not Jesus' disciples, but they certainly laid claim to being the true "sheep" of God's pasture. In His last excoriating rebuke of these hypocrites, the Lord accused them of "shut[ting] up the kingdom of heaven against men," neither entering in themselves nor allowing anyone else to do so (Matt 23.13). He called them "blind leaders" of the blind (Matt 15.14) and warned His disciples away from their teaching (Matt 16.6–12). Jesus' warning is certainly not limited in application to the Pharisees and their ilk, but it begins there and reaches out to encompass all who would pervert the gospel and obscure the narrow gate.

The second clear assumption of our Savior's admonition about "false prophets" is that there is an objective standard by which those who come claiming to speak the will of God may be judged true or false. The same presupposition guided the teaching of Moses who warned that even those prophets who dealt with apparent signs and wonders were to be labeled deceivers when they called on Israel to disobey God's already revealed will (Deut 13.1–4). The false prophets were those who spoke "a vision of their own heart, not from the mouth of the LORD" (Jer 23.16). Jesus, like Moses, is no syncretist, drawing radically conflicting beliefs together and calling them all equally true. He has already identified the false teacher in this sermon as anyone who breaks His Father's least commandment and teaches others to do likewise (Matt 5.19). The existential spirit of these times makes men draw back from absolutes. "Truth," for them, is all a matter of personal taste. But the spirit of the Great Teacher is unyieldingly exclusive. He alone, He says, is the revelation of the Truth and no one can find God apart from Him (John 1.18; 14.6). His Father's will (Matt 7.21), His own words (Matt 7.24), are to be the standard of judgment. Teachers in our time or in any other who say that "there are many roads to God" have not been sent by the only begotten Son. They are false. They are deceivers.

Looking Under the Sheepskin

A third assumption behind Jesus' warning about false teachers is that they are dangerous. These pseudo-prophets are not just momentarily misguided individuals. They are corrupt to the core, false in the very essence of their spiritual lives ("*inwardly* they are ravenous wolves"). Like the bestial prince who rules them (1 Pet 5.8), their purpose is not to serve but to devour. They do not nurture their followers, they consume them (Acts 20.29–30; 2 Pet 2.3).

But the real danger of these false prophets lies in their skillful deceit. They come "in sheep's clothing." Their true character and intent are always cloaked in an appearance of piety. They pose as disciples. The ignorant and unwary who deal in careless superficialities are destined to be deceived by these slick operators who, far from being openly carnal and repulsive, are, as Paul describes them, religiously attractive (2 Cor 11.13), worldly-wise (Col 2.8), and charming (Rom 16.17–18). They are just the sort of people who would move shallow-minded observers to ask how these good, earnest and knowledgeable teachers could be wrong. If we are to walk securely in the narrow way, it is not enough to be harmless; we must also be wise (Matt 10.16).

"You will know them by their fruits…" (Matt 7.16). The Lord's warning about false prophets was bound to send a chill of fear through the hearts of the disciples. In the *world*, the kingdom of God had enemies aplenty. That was not news. But here was threat from within—from their own close and intimate comrades! How could they know whom to trust? How tell the false from the true?

The fear of pseudo-disciples has moved some Christians to paranoia. They sense false teachers behind every bush and are constantly in a questioning and investigative mood. But there is nothing in Jesus' words to make His disciples constitutionally suspicious, even cynical, toward all their brethren. It is at the level of *fruit* that these judgments are to be made and not before the sprout is even out of the ground. As Bonhoeffer says: "There is no need to go prying into the hearts of others. All we need do is wait until the tree bears fruit, and we shall not have to wait long" (*The Cost of Discipleship*, p 146).

For this reason, we need not hesitate to be fair with the teachers who come our way, giving them the benefit of the doubt until circumstances are clear. This will not make us trustingly simple or turn us into fresh meat for every deceiver. The fruit will reveal the tree soon enough. And it is likely better to be momentarily deceived by an occasional wolf than to be constantly and impetuously trying to jerk the wool off of every one of the Lord's sheep.

Still, judgments are going to have to be made and warnings issued when the fruit of false teachers comes to harvest. Though the Lord's prohibition of judging others (Matt 7.1) rules out a harsh and unfair judgmentalism, it certainly does not forbid the testing of teachers and so-called prophets. The spirits must be proven to determine "whether they are of God" (1 John 4.1). The Lord's counsel here is not the same as in the parable of the Tares (Matt 13.36–43). It has nothing to do with attempting ultimate divine judgment on men and therefore need not be reserved to God and the hereafter. Jesus is simply giving prudent counsel about how false teachers can be recognized and avoided. Day-to-day events would reveal them. All disguises eventually slip. Pretenses cannot be kept up forever. Trees will bear fruit.

But what will be the nature of the deception of these prophets and what is the fruit by which they are to be tested?

The false prophets of the Old Testament era were men about whom all spoke well (Luke 6.26). Their preaching was always comforting, even when circumstances demanded warning and chastening (Jer 6.14). They prophesied lies (Jer 27.9–10), but they were always appealing lies which served their own selfish purposes (Mic 3.11).

Jesus' present warning reveals that things are not to be different in the gospel age. False prophets were to speak knowing lies (1 Tim 4.2) in order to meet the market for comforting deception (2 Tim 4.3–4). Heedless of the real needs of God's people, these teachers would tell them what they wanted to hear. Such preachers are likely to make little or no mention of God's righteousness, the horror of sin, the need for true repentance, or hell (Acts 24.25). They will not declare "the whole counsel of God" (Acts 20.27). There will be no "narrow way" in their preaching.

But what is the fruit of these "corrupt trees"? The very fact that they are called "false prophets" shows that the fruit of their mouths is corrupt—false. Their teaching will fail the test of God's word (Acts 17.11). But since the mouth speaks "out of the abundance of the heart" (Matt 12.34), the evil at the fountainhead is bound to reveal itself in character as well as teaching.

The best defense against these deceivers is to love the Lord supremely and cherish His word. Those who are earnestly seeking the narrow way and strait gate will not be drawn away by these self-serving hypocrites.

Life Reveals the Heart

False prophets are at last not simply wrong in their teaching, but also in their hearts. Dishonesty with the gospel message is bound to create dishonesty in life. The inner forces which produce the deviant message in the first place (pride of life, fear of men, love of money, lust of the flesh, *et al.*). will inevitably manifest themselves in behavior, however subtly. This is the reason that Jesus' warning about false prophets leads so naturally to a discussion of testing them by their character as well as their message. Presumed prophets must first be tested at the level of their teaching. What they have to say should be compared with the gospel proclaimed "from the beginning" (1 John 1.1–3; 2.18–24; 4.1–3; Gal 1.6–8) and, failing the comparison, be rejected (2 John 9–10). From the vantage point of our own times, all teachers who come claiming divine revelation should, in view of the long since completed disclosure of God's will in Christ (John 16.12–13; 2 Tim 3.16–17; 2 Pet 1.3; Jude 3) and the consequent termination of the prophetic office (1 Cor 13.8), be rejected out of hand. But, finally, the fruit of the corrupt tree will be borne and its nature revealed. False teachers cannot be good men. The ungodly may, at times, preach a pure gospel, but false teachers are incapable of living truly godly lives.

Jesus' analogy from nature—the tree is known by its fruit—drives home the point that kingdom citizenship is not a matter of appearance, but of being. People, like trees, produce the kind of fruit that their nature demands. Therefore, being a Christian is not simply a matter of *doing* something new, but of *being* something new. It is the kind of life which begins in the heart, at the center of the personality. That is the reason it is only produced by a new birth (John 3.3–5). Some have attempted to follow Christ by adding some new dimension to their lives when it is the life itself which must be changed. You can tie grapes on thorns and figs on thistles, but they will not grow there. A wolf may wear wool, but he cannot produce it. The true child of the kingdom is different. As Jesus said, "out of *his heart* will flow rivers of living water" (John 7.38). Sin in all its manifestations begins in the heart (Matt 15.19) and it is consequently in the heart and from the heart that a new kind of fruit must be borne.

It is because of the inner nature of true godliness that the testing of teachers and of disciples generally must always be a search beneath the skin. There is a righteousness and a piety that arises, not from a humble faith in the Son of God, but from pride and the desire for moral and spiritual excellence. The subtle, but unconcealable, flaw of this kind of "spirituality" is the utter absence in it of the qualities of the beatitudes—the meekness, compassion and selflessness, the godly sorrow for sin. There will also be about this attractive religious patina an inability to produce the fruit of the Spirit—"love, joy, peace, longsuffering, kindness, ...gentleness, self-control..." (Gal 5.22–23).

It is for this very reason that John, wrestling in his epistles with the Gnostic teachers who threatened with their perversions to overwhelm the churches, urges not only a doctrinal test of teachers, but an ethical one. Like many religious movements that have arisen since, Gnosticism flourished because it caught the spirit of the age with its claim to a deep spirituality which transcended all moral and ethical questions. The Gnostic teachers offered a new and improved gospel which did not suffer the contempt of the world at large and gave release from the agonizing questions of practical righteousness. Their success was shaking the confidence of faithful saints both in the gospel and in their own salvation. In response, John speaks plainly: "He who says, 'I know him,' and does not keep His commandments, is a liar" (1 John 2.4); "He who says he is in the light, and hates his brother, is in darkness" (1 John 2.9); "In this the children of God and the children of the devil are manifest: Whoever does not practice righteousness is not of God, nor is he who does not love his brother. For this is the message that you heard from the beginning" (1 John 3.10–11).

But what about the great popularity of these preachers and of their message? Doesn't that show them to be true prophets? John again answers bluntly: "They are of the world. Therefore they speak as of the world, and the world hears them" (1 John 4.5).

Christians need to pray for the discernment, wisdom and faith not to be deceived by false teachers who cover their error with an apparent, but superficial, godliness. They need also to seek deliverance from the "success" mentality which sees every carnal advance as testimony to the truth of its message while the commands of God are abandoned both in preaching and in life. To disciples struggling laboriously with an antagonistic world and the unholy desires that rise even within their own personalities, such prophets of a "new gospel" will always have a powerful appeal—but the appeal is of the darkness, not the light. "Beware of false prophets." "You will know them by their fruits."

What the Kingdom of God Is All About

"Not everyone who says to Me, 'Lord, Lord,' shall enter the kingdom of heaven, but he who does the will of My Father in heaven" (Matt 7.21). As is evident from this pointed warning, superficial discipleship is not a twentieth-century invention. Jesus was plagued by it almost from the outset of His public preaching (John 2.23–24). The ranks of enthusiastic but heedless "groupies" seemed to grow in tandem with His early popularity, and He was constantly at pains to shake them into a sober awareness of what following Him meant (Luke 14.25–35). Yet even these were but the natural heirs of the Pharisees, and the mindless ritualists who, centuries before, had called forth the passionate and frequently scathing rebuke of the Old Testament prophets (Isa 1.11–17; Amos 5.21–24).

With language that has become even more piercingly plain, Jesus turns from the false prophets to the false professors and their false standards. It is dangerous enough for a man to take the broad road to destruction on purpose, but it is infinitely more dangerous for him to take it, believing it is the way to life. Enthusiastic shouts of "Lord, Lord" can be nothing more than a convenient bit of fleece to cover an unyielding heart. There may not be a wolf beneath this sheepskin, but there certainly is a goat! Empty professions are as dangerous to the narrow road as false prophets.

There is nothing untoward about an earnest confession of faith in the Son of God and the open acknowledgment that He is Lord. Indeed, there can be no true discipleship without it (Matt 10.32–33; Rom 10.9–10). But the tragedy sets in when that is all there is—a mouthy declaration of Jesus' sovereignty without any evidence of submission (Luke 6.46).

Who are these bold confessors? They are not knowing hypocrites, for Jesus says they will not understand His rejection of them in the final judgment (Matt 7.22). They are not lazy ne'er-do-wells because Jesus does not challenge their claim to zealous activity in His name. Their problem is a simple one. In all their saying and doing, they had not done the one thing that He expected of them and that was to do His Father's will.

On this point those who aspire to walk the narrow road must be very clear. In the kingdom of God, nothing will be received as a substitute for obedience! Certainly not the mere confession of the mouth. Absolutely not the diligent practice of religious ordinances which originate with man rather than God (Mark 7.1–8). No, not even the faithful observance of certain select commands of God while others are being studiously neglected or disobeyed (Matt 23.23). And, at last, there will not even be acceptance while only one out of all God's commands is being stubbornly refused, ignored or perverted (Mark 10.17–22; Jas 2.8–11).

This has nothing to do with justification by works. It has to do with single-minded faith, undivided loyalty, and absolute trust. There will always be mercy from the Lord for those whose heart is fully set on pleasing Him in all things, for they will always be willing to learn more, seek forgiveness, and do better. But for the man who picks and chooses his way through the divine will, not all the zealous religious activity which can be mounted will suffice to cover the failure.

"Many will say to Me in that day, 'Lord, Lord, have we not prophesied in Your name, cast out demons in Your name, and done many wonders in Your name?'" (Matt 7.22). The fact that those disobedient confessors make the unchallenged claim not only to have possessed, but to have exercised, miraculous gifts by the power of Christ suggests that they were disciples. Many have felt that their claims had to be false, but not necessarily.

Whatever his immense failings as a man, Balaam certainly prophesied by the power of God (Num 22.35; 23.16). There can be little doubt that Judas Iscariot, as one of the Twelve, employed miraculous powers (Matt 10.1). Carnal disciples at Corinth certainly did (1 Cor 1.4–7; 3.1–3). Spiritual gifts never were a guarantee of the spirituality or divine acceptance of the teacher, only that the message was true.

So we, too, may preach the true gospel to many people and "do many mighty works," but at last be rejected simply because we did not obey the Lord (1 Cor 9.27; 13.1–3; Phil 1.15–17). These self-deluded professors were asking the wrong question. The great work that God had done by them was not in and of itself consequential for their salvation; whether they had truly served and pleased the Lord was (Luke 10.20).

The Final Humiliation

"And then I will declare to them, 'I never knew you; depart from Me, you who practice lawlessness!'" (Matt 7.23). The scene that Jesus sets in these final somber words is of a group of enthusiasts who have bandied His name about freely and made much ado about their intimate ties to Him. From the warm and reverential way they must have spoken of the Son of God, observers would doubtless have judged them to be among His most devout disciples. There certainly would have been frequent and fervent declaration that they knew the Lord. It was their spiritual talisman, the charm that gave them assurance.

And it was at this very point where they were most boastful and at a time and place when it would be most hopelessly devastating that Jesus promises to make His own profession. In the presence of all assembled humanity, including every person who ever heard them claim Him as their own, He will say, *"I never knew you"!* The absolute humiliation of such a moment for such people would be almost indescribable.

In Luke, the Lord paints a similar picture of men crying for recognition at the final judgment (Luke 13.22–30). But here it is directed toward those whose dread of the "narrow door" makes them unwilling even to say, "Lord, Lord," much less to do His will. The basis of their claim is not that they had acknowledged Him as Master or given Him service, but that they had been socially acquainted. He had taught in their streets and eaten at their tables. Here is a picture even more startling than that of the bold professors—people who for a whole lifetime had openly rejected the Son of God and yet were still hoping, even believing, that He would not reject *them.* This gives new dimensions to the human capacity for self-deception. As amazing as it may seem, there are multitudes of men and women today who feel that their repudiation of the Holy One of God has been accomplished with such politeness and civility that it will not cost them anything in eternity.

In Matthew, unlike Luke, Jesus is dealing with those who count themselves disciples. The fact that the Lord says to them, "I *never* knew you," does not necessarily mean that they had never been genuine, but that throughout the time they were performing their vaunted "mighty works" in His name their disobedience had made them strangers to Him. At last, for all their declarations and ardent labors, they were no better off than those who had pointedly rejected the Son of God.

Jesus does not treat these pleading claimants who have attempted to trade zeal for submission gently. "Workers of iniquity" He calls them, as if to awaken His immediate hearers to the fact that, however subtle, this kind of piety-cloaked rebellion is serious and its condemnation just. The same word here translated lawlessness (Greek *anomia*) is used again by Matthew in recording the Lord's last excoriating rebuke of the Pharisees. Like whitewashed tombs, they had an appearance of righteousness but were inwardly "full of hypocrisy and *lawlessness*" (Matt 23.27–28). John employs it to describe the very nature and genius of sin—"lawlessness" or "unrighteousness" (1 John 3.4).

But if these sham disciples are lawless, they are not necessarily "antinomian" (denying God has a law). For them, it is a matter (at some point) of knowingly refusing to submit to the will of God. They are not people who sin by oversight or weakness, but by design. Those who sin by weakness are not given to pretended piety, but to humility and repentance. They know all too well what sin costs and they want none of it. Jesus sets the deeds of these pretenders over against those that "do the will of My Father."

As has already been noted, the setting of this prospective conversation is one of final judgment where ultimate destinies are being decided. The Lord's heart-piercing "Depart from Me, you who practice lawlessness" can make the Genesis picture of God driving His rebel creatures out of Eden seem almost bright. There was a remedy for that tragedy. For this one, there is none. Sin is always a separating force, working alienation from oneself and from others, but sin's ultimate horror is banishment without re-course from the very presence of God. With what difficulty we struggle to imagine what it would be like never to look upon the face of love, goodness or purity ever again, either at their divine source or as reflected in men who have been touched by them. More than a year later and using similar language, Jesus will de-scribe the experience as being cast into "everlasting fire" (Matt 25.41). May none of us ever learn how the reality of that moment beggars these words.

The Danger of Self-Deception

We have already spoken briefly about the serious self-deception required to cause religious men and women to quarrel with the Son of God even as He sits on His judgment throne. Matthew 7.21–23 does not describe people who are playing a knowing game. The presence of God in His glory would tend to take away a man's appetite for pretense. What these verses reveal is the ability of a human being to hide his own motives and choices from himself. The important question they raise is: How do we get ourselves into such a state of self-delusion, and how can we avoid it?

The revelation in these verses that the day of judgment will be a day of surprises is not a little startling. Won't men know in their heart of hearts that they have not been faithful to the Lord? How could they not realize their disobedience? These are not untaught people, strangers to the gospel of the kingdom. How could they not know? The answer: self-deception.

Self-deception is based on self-justification, the use of the wrong standard by which to judge oneself (Luke 16.15; 18.9–17) or the simple failure to use the true standard (God's word).

The seriousness of the threat it presents to seekers after the kingdom of God is evidenced by the number of warnings against it. Paul says that men deceive themselves when they think themselves wise or imagine themselves to be something when they are nothing (1 Cor 3.18; Gal 6.30.) Pride and vanity can lead one to believe lies about himself which he himself has told! James, in his very direct way, warns that it is a self-deluded person who thinks he will get credit for listening to the word of God which he never practices, and illustrates his point with the man who thinks himself very pious while exercising no control over his tongue (Jas 1.22–26). Much church-going can give false assurance to those who had rather talk about true religion than live it. Preaching sound doctrine doesn't necessarily make one godly. Finally, John admonishes that when we deny there is any sin at all in our lives, we are lying to ourselves (1 John 1.8). The psychic pain of confessing failure often moves us to seek cover for our sins in religious activism rather than repentance and confession.

And why do men work so diligently to convince not just others, but themselves, of these myths about their relationship to God? Because they find the truth that God has spoken to them wholly unappealing and, determined to reject it, do not want to bear the pain of living with a constantly aching and accusing conscience (2 Thes 2.10–12; 1 Tim 4.1–2). Something must be found to fill the void and justify their disobedience.

A distorted view of "justification by faith" has been a popular subterfuge. Boiled down, this approach holds that Christ has no concern with how you live, only how you feel. From this vantage point, too great a concern for obedience to God's commands is seen as a denial of God's grace and a rejection of the gospel. At times, it almost echoes the libertine spirit which Paul condemns in Romans 6.1–2: "Let us sin the more that grace may abound!" The more proponents of this idea are reproved for their transgression of divine will, the more they declare their confidence in God's grace and the power of their faith. But this is not faith *in God,* but "faith in faith"—a self-serving "believism." We are certainly justified by faith, but a faith that manifests itself by obedience to God's commands (Luke 6.46; John 14.15, 21, 23; 15.10, 14; Gal 5.6; Jas 2.14–26). That is clearly the message of the Sermon on the Mount.

Another frequent cover for disobedience is "the end justifies the means." What difference does it make how it was done, the argument goes, as long as a desirable result is obtained? This may have been the logic of David when moving the ark of the covenant to Jerusalem. The end was good, but the means were rejected dramatically (1 Chron 13.1–14; 15.1–15). It was certainly the thinking of Saul when he disobeyed God in the slaughter of the Amalekites. The sparing of the best animals (a transgression) was justified as a means of worshipping God (1 Sam 15.15). God was not impressed (1 Sam 15.22–23). If there is a clear point made in the Sermon on the Mount, and there are many, it is that in the kingdom of heaven, means and end are one. Divinely chosen means are suited to divinely never produce the submissive, trusting heart which our Lord longs after.

But, how are we to escape this human proclivity for self-delusion? By approaching the Scripture with our hearts given to God and not with an academic or institutional interest. We must face up to what the Son of God has actually said, regardless of whether it is costly or painful or out of fashion. And then, in the clear light of the Lord's teaching, we must engage constantly in the most earnest probing of our own hearts (2 Cor 13.5). Without self-examination, self-deception is inevitable. We have to ask ourselves not only if what we are doing is according to God's will, but if we are doing it for love of His Son. Altogether too much done "in the name of Christ" is performed for the glory of men. How imperative in us is the spirit of David: "Search me, O God, and know my heart; try me, and know my anxieties; and see if there is any wicked way in me, and lead me in the way everlasting" (Psa 139.23–24).

Building a Life that Will Last

The preacher has preached His sermon, and His invitation to action, already begun, is now concluded. The road has been forking continuously throughout the discourse: two kinds of righteousness, two kinds of treasure, a broad and a narrow way, hypocrisy or simplicity, this world or the next, our will or God's. The choice has been clearly and powerfully drawn.

It is not looking good or sounding pious or doing "something wonderful" in Jesus' name that takes one to the kingdom of God. It is obedience—obedience as an expression of absolute trust. In His concluding appeal, the Lord has already painted two pictures to illustrate this fact. He now gives His hearers the third and last.

"Therefore whoever hears these sayings of Mine, and does them, I will liken him to a wise man who built his house on the rock: and the rain descended, the floods came, and the winds blew and beat on that house; and it did not fall, for it was founded on the rock. But everyone who hears these sayings of Mine, and does not do them, will be like a foolish man who built his house on the sand: and the rain descended, the floods came, and the winds blew and beat on that house; and it fell. And great was its fall" (Matt 7.24–27).

The Two Builders. In these verses, the Lord introduces us to two builders. We can discover the difference in them by observing the similarities. Both these men had the same wish—to build a house—a place to live, a place of shelter and security. Each built his house and if the two were dissimilar, it is not noted. Both houses were tested by the same storm. At last, the only discernible difference in these two builders and their houses is the foundation on which they chose to build—one on the rock, the other on the sand. And before the deluge fell, both men seemed to have succeeded admirably.

This story suggests that whatever the house is, all men are seeking to build it. It could be called "success" or "happiness" or "peace of mind" or "fulfillment." It stands for the common longings of the human heart, longings which are not necessarily wrong in themselves but a part of the way God made us. "He has put eternity in their hearts" (Ecc 3.11).

The differing foundations stand for the *way* we try to fulfill our desire for happiness. So far as the Son of God is concerned, there are only two foundations on which to rest our aspirations for ultimate fulfillment—submitting to His will, or rebelling against it. The first house will stand, the second will fall.

The Two Foundations. The wise builder took the time to dig to solid footing (Luke 6.48). It was laborious and time-consuming, but his house and all he was to put into it, even his own life, were at stake. He took the long look and considered more than present sunny skies. It was the inevitable storm for which he built.

The fool built for the moment and without foresight. Whatever could be done with little effort and achieve quick results attracted him. He presumed that the way things were was the way they would always be. The idea that his house might be severely tested appears never to have entered his mind. He doubtless had his house up and furnished before his struggling neighbor had even completed his foundation.

Building Before the Storm. It is important to realize that in our Lord's story there is a time when any differences in these two builders will be hard to see. Both will appear to have succeeded—houses standing firm and unshaken. In fact, the fool, having saved himself so many rigors, may seem even to have the better of it. And it is in the midst of this time, before the storm, that we must decide how to build our own spiritual houses. Of course, it will be easy enough to see the difference after the tempest, but that will be too late to mean anything. It is now, in the calm before the cataclysm, that we must act *out of faith*. We must prepare for the deluge in dry weather. We must run from Sodom before even the first sign of the firestorm.

To the careless eye, the practical difference between the children of God and the children of this world will be difficult to see. Both will suffer reverses, know heartaches, fall ill, and die. For this reason thoughtless people will always struggle to see the distinction between true righteousness and Pharisaic hypocrisy—between the narrow way and the broad one—between the true prophet and the zealous impostor. That is the reason that an attitude of humility and honesty is so vital for those who want to survive the storm of divine judgment. We must have the meekness of spirit which will enable us to see ourselves for what we are, and the Son of God for who He is.

The day is coming when the differences which tend to escape the attention of the unthinking will be starkly evident. Speaking of that day of reckoning in His explanation of the parable of the Tares, Jesus promises that "then the righteous will shine forth as the sun in the kingdom of their Father" (Matt 13.43). Even the blindest of men will see the difference then. We need the eyes to see it *now*, and to order our lives accordingly.

Where to Build Your Life

In His very final words (Matt 7.24–27), with a notable absence of anything high-sounding or ornate (it would not have suited the style of the Teacher or His sermon), Jesus urges His hearers to consider soberly the consequences of the response they choose to give Him. Indifference and neutrality are not an option. All men will build. The only question left is where. He confronts the listener squarely, leaving no room for maneuvering. Will they submit to His will and do what He says or no? The choice is theirs, but it is a radical choice with radical repercussions.

The issue throughout the sermon has been one of obedience. The voice that speaks is not simply the voice of truth and wisdom, but the voice of authority and power. Submission must be both wide and deep—as wide as His least commandment (Matt 5.19–48) and as deep as our innermost thoughts (Matt 6.1–34).

And to whom are these words specially addressed? Not to the heathen and the publican, for they have received almost no attention in this great discourse. The "therefore" with which Jesus begins this last thrust of His sermon tells us that He is drawing a conclusion from what He has just said about pseudo-prophets and false professors (Matt 7.15–23). These words, as indeed the whole sermon, are addressed to those who make a pretense of discipleship. They confront that shallow religiosity, offered as a substitute for obedience, which was then plaguing the nation of Israel, and is wreaking havoc in our times. The "wise man" is not "the man who hears these words" and understands them—not even the man who hears and believes in the Son of God. The people the Lord is addressing had already heard, and "believed," and in some measure understood, but the question on which everything hinged was whether they had obeyed. There is nothing that this sermon strikes more at the heart of than the constant quoting of John 3.16

by those who studiously avoid the study and practice of the word of the very One on whom they profess to believe. It is a mockery!

Of course, the fact that this sermon and these particular words are directed specially toward sham disciples does not mean that they have no application to those who do not make the least pretense of following Jesus. Whether a pretender or a prodigal, the consequences of rebellion are the same. Sand is sand.

The Unshakable Rock. The wise man, says Jesus, is the man who hears the word from heaven and does it—no questions asked, no excuses given. Because of an obedient faith, his relationship with both Father and Son is as unshakable as a huge ledge of rock (Greek *petra)* in a storm. The Son of God gave the same assurance in Jerusalem the December before He died when He said of His "sheep" that "follow Me" and "hear My voice," no one shall "snatch them out of My hand" (John 10.27–29). Paul echoed Jesus when he assured the Romans that as for those that love the Lord and are called according to His purpose, *nothing* shall separate them "from the love of God which is in Christ Jesus our Lord" (Rom 8.28–39). It is the "obedience to the faith" (Rom 1.5; 16.26) as a living and constant principle of life that sticks us to the Savior of men in an unbreakable union. As Isaiah promised, the Lord God has laid His foundation in Zion, a "precious cornerstone, a sure foundation" and "whoever believes on Him will not be put to shame" (Isa 28.16; Rom 9.33).

It is important to remind ourselves again at this point that Jesus is not dealing here with the ground of our salvation (grace), but with the nature of the faith that responds to it. James is but repeating the Sermon on the Mount when he warns us to be "doers of the word, and not hearers only" (Jas 1.22) and declares that "faith by itself, if it does not have works, is dead" (Jas 2.17, 26). Why act as though James is an innovator here? It is Jesus who first preached this principle and He did it in the "gospel of the kingdom" (Matt 4.23). This foundational truth needs desperately to go home. Those who have become so fascinated with salvation *by grace* that they have emptied faith of all content need to realize that they are flirting not with inconvenience, but destruction. There is an abundance of mercy upon every soul who submits to the rule of Christ with his whole heart—his heart will break and turn again with every transgression—but there will be no compassion for those who headily determine that grace has made the commands of the Lord of the kingdom of none effect.

Rock or Sand?

Jesus has called for an obedience to His word which is both profound and all-encompassing, but it is not an invitation to justification by works of righteousness. He urges kingdom citizens to seek the perfection of their Father's selfless love (Matt 5.43–48), but says plainly that they will yet need to repent of their wrongs (Matt 5.23) and seek mercy (Matt 5.7). On the occasion of His death, when Jesus commends the Twelve to His Father as men who "have kept Your word" (John 17.6), He is not saying that they have been sinless since becoming His disciples (their record proves otherwise), but that their commitment to Him has been genuine and their penitent grief for their sins unalloyed.

Those who build their lives upon "the rock" are saying two things: that they are determined to keep the word of Christ at all costs, and that they are trusting His redemptive blood for mercy upon their failures. Obedience, in the kingdom of heaven, has never been a means of justification from sin, but a way to express faith (Jas 2.14–26) and love (John 14.15, 21, 23; 15.10, 14). If there is any other way to demonstrate these two indispensable qualities of kingdom life they are unknown to Scripture.

In spite of the clarity of the choice the Lord has set before His hearers, there are always those who want to build on sand and call it rock. They are in search of quick and easy solutions to their problems and a facile path to righteousness and peace. It is such minds which tend to turn the Lord's churches toward a more popular and digestible message—one that takes the hard edge off gospel demands and substitutes psychological nostrums that have no bite—and no power. Instead of a penetrating call for a reborn heart, there is only endless prattle about "positive mental attitudes," "self-esteem" and "self-acceptance." A sense of self-worth and a positive spirit are not matters of little consequence, but they will not be had by seeking them for themselves. They are the natural by-product of penitently seeking God and His will and the consequent assurance of acceptance in His grace (Acts 10.34; 2 Cor 8.12; Eph 1.6–7, KJV).

The loss of self-esteem comes most often from a failure to seek the Lord sincerely and obediently. It is hard for a person to look himself in the eye when he knows he is not being genuine toward God. The true grace of Christ brings submission and assurance. Cheap and undemanding grace only serves to deceive the shallow.

It is astonishing that this great sermon with its tremendous emphasis on understanding and obeying the commandments of God has not had a greater impact on the popular Christian mind. Perhaps the reason for this lies in the widely held idea that since we are "not under law but under grace" (Rom 6.14) the commands of Christ are mere guidelines (grace), whereas the commands of Moses were statutes to be strictly obeyed (law). That this is a perversion of Paul is made evident from the amazed question with which he follows his statement about grace and law: "Shall we sin because we are not under law but under grace? Certainly not!" (Rom 6.15). The truth is that God has never since Adam uttered a command which He did not expect to be obeyed. His will rises out of His righteous and gracious nature and is "for our good always" (Deut 6.24; 1 John 5.3).

The grace of God is not lawless. The gospel is simply a *system* of grace (where there is forgiveness for transgressions of God's law) as opposed to a *system* of law (where there is none). Not only does grace not remove the demands of divine law, but it works to meet those demands by a redemptive sacrifice (Rom 8.1–4). Without God's law, His grace would be rendered meaningless, since the absence of law would make sin impossible (Rom 4.15) and forgiveness unnecessary.

Man has been under divine law since Adam, a law best summed up in the commands to love God supremely and one's neighbor as oneself (Matt 22.35–40). Yet that law has never nullified justification by faith, a redemption made possible in all generations because of what God purposed to do in Christ (Heb 9.15). The fact that Abel was justified by faith and showed that faith by a careful obedience to divine law demonstrates that salvation by grace does not alter one's responsibility to obey God (Heb 11.4). The fact that Noah was justified by faith and manifested that faith by a scrupulous submission to divine commands speaks to the same truth (Heb 11.7). The cases of Abraham (Heb 11.8–9, 17–19) and Moses (Heb 11.25–27) add further evidence.

If, then, justification by faith in ages past did not remove the need to obey the commands of God as given, the same necessity must rule in the gospel age. The grace of God in Christ does not free us from the need to obey the Lord, but enables us to obey Him without fear of judgment. And by this very means we are not only forgiven, but transformed (Rom 8.1, 29). This is the message of the Sermon on the Mount. The Preacher has left us between the rock and the sand, between obedient trust and faithless rejection, and challenged us to choose.

"And Great Was Its Fall"

The breathless hush which settled upon that Galilean hillside as Jesus ended His remarkable sermon must have been intense. His words had been startling, and unsettling. Conventional wisdom had been contradicted and long-held traditions rejected. The kingdom of God was not to be revealed in some Philistine conquest, but in an absolute love for God and a self-emptying love for man—and the spirit of this love was to be seen in a submissive obedience to the divine will. In the most concrete terms and with radical directness, the Son of God has described the kingdom of heaven as it truly is, and then challenged His hearers to receive it. Matthew does not tell us how the disciples responded, but "the people were astonished at His teaching" (Matt 7.28).

The Lord's last words are somber. They speak of ultimate ruin—disaster of unspeakable proportions—for those who choose to reject His words and the reign of God among men. There is no consoling universalism in the Sermon on the Mount. All are not to be saved at last. As much as this great discourse speaks of ultimate peace and happiness, it also speaks most clearly, and finally, of the possibility of consummate loss and misery. It is this quality of the gospel of the kingdom that makes its message so urgent, and so grave.

The attachment that universalist minds feel for this sermon is beyond explanation. Do they focus on the Savior's great ethical teachings and simply ignore the rest? Never, in all the Bible, have more ominous warnings of judgment been uttered than those spoken on that now famous hillside in Galilee. Nor are they restricted to a narrow corner of the Lord's message. The prospect of divine rejection threads its way through the whole sermon. For those who refuse to do His Father's will from the heart, Jesus promises not merely the loss of all heavenly reward (Matt 6.1–2, 5, 16), but severe judgment—judgment that is without mercy (Matt 6.15; 7.1–2). The Lord describes the disobedient as traveling the road to "destruction" (Matt 7.13) and in danger of "hell fire" (Matt 5.22, 29–30; 7.19).

It is for this reason that Jesus characterizes the destiny of the rebellious, whether out-and-out worldlings or religious hypocrites, as a "great" ruin and a "great" fall (Luke 6.49; Matt 7.27). The loss of God is not to be a quiet slipping away into oblivion, but a knowing and unending alienation from all that God is—love, compassion, purity, holiness, righteousness, truth—and the attendant wretchedness which such a horror produces (Matt 13.41–42, 49–50; 25.46). It will be the *chosen* destiny of those who turn away from God's love and way, to spend eternity with all of the shame, hypocrisy, arrogance, selfishness, lust, hate and brutality of human history (1 Cor 6.9–10; Gal 5.19–21; 2 Thes 1.7–9; Rev 14.11; 21.8; 22.10–15). The depth of such a moral darkness, the intensity of such a spiritual fire, beggars description. In that "outer darkness" with its "everlasting fire" there shall indeed be "weeping and gnashing of teeth" (Matt 25.30, 41).

Does it have to be stated that in spite of these dark words of warning that the whole thrust of the Lord's work and preaching was to deliver men from such an unspeakable fate? If His preaching seems at times abrupt, it is only to awaken us from the mindless religious routines through which we sleepwalk our way. Jesus calls us to a vital relationship with His Father. It is a relationship which makes us truly alive, permeating thought and act, transforming character and personality, making us beyond all question the children of the *living* God.

The greatness of God's love ought to be sufficient cause to bring us into glad submission to His righteous and gracious rule, but the reality of our nature is that often nothing save the thunder of divine judgment can open our ears to His voice. And it is with this in mind that the One who loved us best of all closes the sermon in which more than any other He opens up to human eyes the wonderful ways of heaven.

Never Man So Spake

"And so it was, when Jesus had ended these saying, that the people were astonished at His teaching, for He taught them as one having authority, and not as the scribes" (Matt 7.28–29). Matthew does not report the response of the disciples to Jesus' sermon, but the curious "multitudes," he says, were astonished. And this would not be the only time the Lord's listeners would be transfixed in surprise at the unexpected content and manner of His words. Later, some Jewish officers, sent to arrest Him, would make the mistake of pausing to listen, and then return amazed and empty-handed to their incredulous superiors with no better explanation of their failure than "we never heard a man speak like that before" (John 7.46).

There is nothing mysterious in all this—no strange manipulation of the mind, no spells or trances. It is simply the effect that hearing the voice of God has on human hearts. Jesus appeared in every way to be so ordinary, so usual, a common artisan from the religious backwaters of Galilee, wholly without formal training and background. This fact often made His remarkable words unbelievable to His audiences (Mark 6.2–3; John 7.15) who seemed unwilling to accept His testimony that His teachings came from His Father (John 7.16–17). His words were not accompanied by the kind of fiery display that shook the summit of Sinai and melted the hearts of Israel into terror (Heb 12.18–24). It was only a man speaking. Yet, He was speaking the absolute, unequivocal truth; not simply as one who had learned it, but as one who had experienced it, as one who at last was identical with it (John 1.18; 14.6). This fact alone was bound to give a unique and compelling quality to Jesus' words. He taught them "as one having authority," as one who knew what He was talking about.

The largely mindless scribes, no real students of the law itself and with hardly an original thought, spent their days studying and collating what ancient influential rabbis had said *about* the law. They suspended their arguments from endless strings of rabbinic quotations and fanciful interpretations. In contrast to the floundering speculations of the scribes which had about them the tinny sound of human confusion, the preaching of Jesus resounded with the deep ring of confident truth. It was filled with quotations of the Old Testament ("it is written") and simple declarations of fact ("verily, I say unto you"). And if the scribes cited the interpretations of the ancient rabbis with ease, Jesus even more easily contradicted them. It is inevitable that the voice of God will sound like the voice of God, and the voice of man like the voice of man. Even the sometimes insensitive multitudes who heard the Lord's remarkable sermon could tell the difference, and it "astonished" them.

The words of Jesus and all the prophets whom God has sent to speak to men will always have about them the mark of their origin. Their power is the power of divine wisdom and truth, and all men are destined to feel their influence even when they choose to reject them. "For the word of God is living and powerful ... and is a discerner of the thoughts and intents of the heart" (Heb 4.12).

To the remarkable nature of His words as a source of difference and surprise must surely be added Jesus' profound love and concern for His listeners. While the scribes wrestled merely with words and arguments, the great Teacher reached out in His teaching for people. All too often the religious leaders of Israel saw people as something to be manipulated and used. It must have been apparent that the Son of God had come to transform rather than to manipulate, to bless rather than to use.

The words of Jesus were always challenging and penetrating, but they were refreshing, too. And that is as we might have expected it. For never in human history, before or since, has the voice of God been heard in the world with such absolute fullness of truth and with such a demonstration of its living reality in the flesh of one man. We, too, must confess in amazement that "we never heard a man speak like that."

Beyond the Sermon—The Preacher

At last we are not so much confronted with the compelling and challenging message of this great sermon as we are with the person of the Preacher Himself. The principal question with which it leaves us is not "What do you think of this sermon?" but "What do you think of this Teacher?"

There is perhaps no more blind approach to the Sermon on the Mount than that of religious rationalism which sees in it the moral and spiritual teachings of the "real" Jesus before His story became encrusted with later supernatural claims. They have, therefore, embraced the sermon as a tremendous breakthrough in ethical science achieved by a purely human Christ. As such, it contains for them wise counsel but not a word from God. It is uncanny that otherwise brilliant men could have made such a patently false analysis. The truth is that no teaching in the Gospels presents such a compelling picture of the divine Christ as does this memorable Galilean discourse.

The first hearers were struck with the Teacher's extraordinary air of authority. He was so unlike their speculating scribes. He did not theorize or hesitate. He was neither tentative nor apologetic, but with quiet assurance laid the foundation of a heavenly kingdom. It was not just style, but substance, and there was every reason why He should have spoken with authority.

He was the Christ, the long-promised Messiah who was destined to fulfill the eternal purpose of God. Jesus does not merely say that every "jot and tittle" of the law and the prophets would be fulfilled, affirming the divine origin of the Old Testament Scriptures, but that *He* had come to fulfill them (Matt 5.17–18). This Preacher claims to be the consummation of the ages! He sees Himself as the Alpha and Omega, the end as well as the beginning.

He was Lord and at last to be Judge. This Preacher claims not only to teach men the everlasting truth, but to be the divinely empowered master of their fate. He clearly portrays Himself as the one who will stand at the end of history and preside over the disposition of the souls of all (Matt 7.21–23). It is to Jesus that they must give ultimate account. What an enormous claim to deity this is! And the claim is enlarged by the Lord's concluding statement about the basis of this final judgment. All will hinge on each person's response to *His* word (Matt 7.24–27). The teachings of this Preacher are not prudent counsel for some passing season, but are valid for all time. They will meet us in eternity. He clearly intends that we should understand that.

So, given this, it is no wonder that He could simply say, "Verily, I say unto you" and make it sound altogether right. Those first hearers were astonished; they were dumbfounded. And even after 1900 years, we are astonished, too!

So, as we have surely learned by now, the sermon is great, indeed. The mark of eternal Truth is upon it. But, for all its greatness, the Preacher towers above His sermon. He is the Lord Christ, the Son of God, and is destined to be the Judge of all. If we reject this teaching and this Teacher, we shall do so at our own eternal peril. All of heaven is in the message and in the Man.

And yet for all His immense power and the critical issues that are at stake for both God and man, the sermon does not end with an imperial demand, but with an urgent invitation. Jesus has proclaimed a kingdom which is wholly foreign to the ways of this world and destined always so to be. He has issued a call for spiritual revolution, a revolution of the most sweeping and profound sort which leaves no part of the human heart untouched and untransformed. It is a high calling, but it is a radical one, and we must each decide for ourselves how we will answer this remarkable invitation. And, most sobering of all, we must then bear for all eternity the transcendent consequences of that decision. As the Preacher so often said, "He who has ears, let him hear."

Helpful Books

Some books helpful in the study of the Sermon on the Mount:

Christian Personal Ethics, Carl F. H. Henry, Eerdmans, Grand Rapids, 1957.

Studies in the Sermon on the Mount, D. Martyn Lloyd-Jones, Eerdmans, Grand Rapids, 1972.

The Cost of Discipleship, Dietrich Bonhoeffer, McMillan, New York, 1957.

Christian Counter-Culture—The Message of the Sermon on the Mount, John R. W. Stott, IVP, Leicester, England, 1978.

The Sermon on the Mount, Robert A. Guelich, Word Books, Waco, Texas, 1982.

An Exposition of the Sermon on the Mount, A. W. Pink, Bible Truth Depot, Swengel, PA, 1950.

ALSO FROM DeWARD PUBLISHING:

Beneath the Cross:
Essays and Reflections on the Lord's Supper
Jady S. Copeland and Nathan Ward (editors)

The Lord's Supper is rich with meaning supplied by Old Testament foreshadowing and New Testament teaching. Explore the depths of symbolism and meaning found in the last hours of the Lord's life in *Beneath the Cross*. Filled with short essays by preachers, scholars, and other Christians, this book is an excellent tool for preparing meaningful Lord's Supper thoughts—or simply for personal study and meditation. 329 pages. $14.99 (PB); $24.99 (HB).

The Slave of Christ
Seth Parr

Immerse yourself in a place where sacrifice is reasonable, love and action are sensible, victory is guaranteed, and evangelism explodes. While the sacrifice of Jesus opens the door for us to Heaven, we must work to be conformed into His very image. In The Slave of Christ, uncover what biblical service means and how it can change your life. Energize your spiritual walk and awaken the servant within. 96 pags. $8.99 (PB)

Boot Camp: Equipping Men with Integrity for Spiritual Warfare
Jason Hardin

According to Steve Arterburn, best-selling author of *Every Man's Battle*, "This is a great book to help us men live opposite of this world's model of man."

Boot Camp is the first volume in the IMAGE series of books for men. It serves as a Basic Training manual in the spiritual war for honor, integrity and a God-glorifying life. 237 pages, $13.99 (PB); $24.99 (HB).

HERITAGE
OF FAITH LIBRARY

The **DeWard Publishing Company Heritage of Faith Library** is a growing collection of classic Christian reprints. DeWard has already published or has plans to publish the following authors:

- A. B. Bruce
- Atticus G. Haygood
- H. C. Leupold
- J. W. McGarvey
- William Paley
- Albertus Pieters

Future authors and titles added to this series will be announced on our website.

For a full listing of DeWard Publishing Company books, visit our website:

www.dewardpublishing.com

DEWARD
PUBLISHING COMPANY

CPSIA information can be obtained at www.ICGtesting.com
Printed in the USA
LVOW06s0106081013

355818LV00001B/31/P